ROOTED IN REMEMBERING

SERMONS FOR THE SUNDAYS AFTER PENTECOST (FIRST HALF)

CYCLE A FIRST LESSON TEXTS

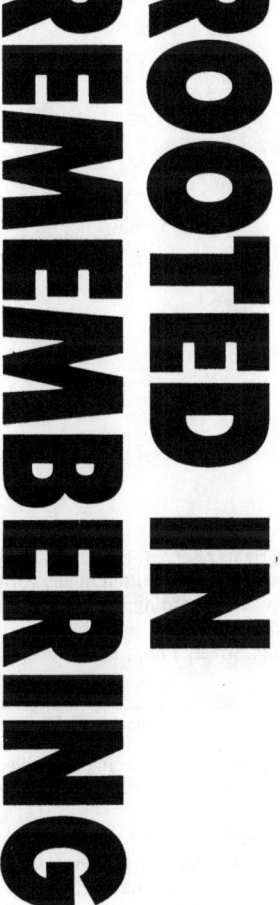

JAMES G. COBB, et al.

C.S.S. Publishing Co., Inc.

Lima, Ohio

ROOTED IN REMEMBERING

Copyright © 1989 by
The C.S.S. Publishing Company, Inc.
Lima, Ohio

All rights reserved. No part of this publication may be reproduced, stored in a retrieval system, or transmitted in any form or by any means, electronic, mechanical, photocopying, recording, or otherwise, without the prior permission of the publisher. Inquiries should be addressed to: The C.S.S. Publishing Company, Inc., 628 South Main Street, Lima, Ohio 45804.

Library of Congress Cataloging-in-Publication Data

Rooted in remembering : a collection of sermons by a family of
   ministers / James G. Cobb, editor.
     p.   cm.
   ISBN 1-55673-133-7
   1. Evangelical Lutheran Church in America — Sermons. 2. Lutheran Church — Sermons. 3. Sermons, American. I. Cobb, James G., 1947-
BX8066.A1R66   1989   89-15771
252'.04135—dc20   CIP

9858 / ISBN 1-55673-133-7   PRINTED IN U.S.A.

In loving memory of
the Rev. William G. and Lillian Akard Cobb
whose love for the Lord and His Church continues
as a legacy to future generations.

Table of Contents

The Day of Pentecost	Isaiah 44:1-8	Pentecost's Promises — Judith Ann Cobb	7
Trinity Sunday	Deuteronomy 4:32-40	A Faith to Live By — John D. Mauney, Jr.	11
Proper 4	Genesis 12:1-9	A Faith-Life to Emulate — John W. Cobb	17
Proper 5	Genesis 22:1-18	But Where Is the Lamb? — John W. Cobb	21
Proper 6	Genesis 25:19-34	Some Crossroads of Family Life — W. Dexter Moser	25
Proper 7	Genesis 27:10-17	Jacob's Dream — A Dream Come True — W. Dexter Moser	31
Proper 8	Genesis 32:22-32	Where Does One Go When Darkness Floods One's Life? —James K. Cobb	39
Proper 9	Exodus 1:6-14, 22:2-10	Expectations of a Vital Faith — James K. Cobb	45
Proper 10	Exodus 2:11-22	A Noble Patriotism — John D. Mauney, Jr.	51
Proper 11	Exodus 3:1-12	A Pilgrimage of Faith — John M. Cobb	59
Proper 12	Exodus 3:13-20	Remembering the Name of God — John W. Cobb	67
Proper 13	Exodus 12:1-14	Remember Toward the Future — John M. Cobb	71
Proper 14	Exodus 14:19-31	Exodus Crossings — James G. Cobb	81

| Proper 15 | Exodus 16:2-15 | **When God Provides, It's a Manna Miracle**
— James G. Cobb | 87 |
| Proper 16 | Exodus 17:1-7 | **The Cry for God**
— James G. Cobb | 93 |

About the Authors 99

Isaiah 44:1-8   The Day of Pentecost

Pentecost's Promises
Judith Ann Cobb

*Fear not . . . for I will pour water on the thirsty
land, and streams on the dry ground;
I will pour my Spirit upon your descendants,
And my blessing on your offspring*
                                        (Isaiah 44:2, 3)

*Thus says the Lord, the King of Israel
And his redeemer, the Lord of Hosts;
"I am the first and I am the last;
Besides Me there is no god."*
                                        (Isaiah 44:6)

We are a people who love promises. We listen for them; we seek them out; and we save them up, but we do not trust them.

We buy appliances with guarantees. Yet more often than not, we discard the guarantee with the box. We know that the appliance will not be permanent and that there will probably be a loophole in the guarantee.

Our life is filled with implicit promises. *If you work hard, you will be a success.* Yet, many who work hard stand in food stamp lines. *If you eat correctly and exercise, you will be healthy;* yet many who seek health are imprisoned in wheelchairs or hospital beds. *If you love, you will be loved.* Yet many who love are abused, divorced, or rejected.

We love promises, but we do not believe them. Even the smallest children doubt the simplest promise when they reply,

"Cross your heart and hope to die? Poke a needle in your eye?" We do not trust promises because we do not believe in permanency. The grass withers, the flowers fade, the world changes, and promises are not forever.

So, why should we believe in God's promises read today in the Isaiah text? What is so special and dependable about this Pentecost's promise from God? These promises are forever. God promised to pour his Spirit upon the descendants and bless the offspring. This promise is binding because he is the first and the last. There is no other. He is permanent.

I often talk with parents before the baptism of their first offspring. They have tell-tale dark circles under their eyes caused by sleepless nights of feeding the child. I tell them to get used to it because the nights of uninterrupted sleep are gone forever. The child will soon awake with earaches, stuffy noses, and fevers. And the parent will rock, bathe, and Tylenol until dawn's early light. Later the child will awaken with the crashes of thunder or bad dreams to scurry into the parents' bed. So, the parents will awaken to nurture and to cuddle until dawn's early light. Still later, the child will awaken with worries about tests and problems. The parents will get up to listen to dawn's early light. And then, so much later the child will never have gone to sleep and the parent will stay awake worrying and watching until the sound of the door closing. There's another dawn's early light.

Our Lord loves us, his own children, so much more than we can even love our children. He promises to pour his Spirit upon his descendants and bless the offspring. He neither slumbers nor sleeps but says, "Ask and it shall be given. Seek and you will find. Knock and it will be opened for you." This one God waits until dawn's early light. This Pentecost promise is forever. He is the first and the last. There is no other.

I spend a lot of time with teens. Some are gathered today on this Pentecost to make an affirmation of their faith in the Rite of Confirmation. They are afraid. They go to school one day and they are liked and popular. The next day, they are "put down" and labeled "nerds." They are under extreme pressure to achieve: win the game, get the grades, earn the money. They wear designer clothes to feel secure. They are freely offered the options of fast driving, free hours, and fantasy escapes into alcohol and other drugs.

They say to me, "How can we make a public profession of our faith promising to continue in the Covenant God made with us in baptism?" I respond that they can make promises because they can always seek the guidance and help of God. I remind them that this is the God who says that since their baptisms they are important no matter what they achieve. This is the God who promises to be there in bread and wine even when they think that they are totally alone. This is the God who calls them one by one to be his disciples. This is the God who will help and guide them.

These are believable promises of this Pentecost. Fear not, I will pour my Spirit upon the descendants and bless the offspring. A Pentecost promise is forever, because he is the first and the last. There is no other.

I spend time with the aged. There are more aged now in this generation than ever before. In our transient society, many are separated from immediate family. Some have outlived their friends and their jobs. They fear uselessness. They fear the "heroics" of medical science as much as they fear death. They've seen a world that has changed from the woodstove to the microwave, from the horseless carriage to the space shuttle, from things sun dried to freeze dried. They view a world that moves fast, and they are not able to run.

And to the aged, the promises of this Pentecost are valuable, because our Lord will pour out his Spirit upon all descendants and his blessings will be a gift to them. Nothing will separate them from the love of God in Christ Jesus — neither things present, nor things past, not things to come. They will never live alone for "if we live, we live to the Lord, and if we die, we die to the Lord. We are the Lord's." (Romans 14:7, 8)

His love is permanent. His promise is permanent.
He is the Lord, the King, the Redeemer.
He is the first and the last.
Beside Him, there is no God.
Pentecost promises, permanent promises, God's promises.

Deuteronomy 4:32-40　　　　　　　Trinity Sunday

A Faith To Live By
John D. Mauney, Jr.

"Know therefore this day, and lay it to your heart, that the Lord is God in the heaven above and on the earth beneath; there is no other."
　　　　　　　　　　　　　　(Deuteronomy 4:39)

We live in a land of plenty. A rich and sophisticated people, we are a nation of greater wealth and technological accomplishment than the world has ever known.

But still there are those among us who are poverty-stricken. We are faced with the age-old problem of the "haves" and the "have-nots." And, of course, there are many different types of poverty. Many Americans are struggling against the problems of material poverty. Witness the ever-growing number of homeless people in our society — such a problem that people like former President Jimmy Carter are expending a tremendous effort to construct homes for those not otherwise able to afford them through a project known as "Habitat for Humanity." And many people among us suffer from a serious lack of education, in such proportions that a large segment of our population is unable to read or write. So we try to develop ways to overcome the problem of illiteracy.

But there is yet another type of poverty not so easily defined — a type difficult to measure against a scale of either material or academic abundance. It is a poverty of morality —

of a sense of values — a poverty that can besmirch even people blessed with great material and educational wealth.

I refer to a poverty of faith in God, a poverty of those convictions basic to Christian living and Christian action. Our convictions are actually an expression of our faith. Just as a growing plant needs sturdy roots to grow strong and healthy, so a Christian needs a carefully determined doctrinal faith as a base upon which to build an effective Christian life that will result in consistent Christian living.

In our text, Moses states precisely and clearly to the people of Israel the basics of the faith upon which they must build their lives. The people of Israel had reached the land of Moab after forty years of journeying in the wilderness and were about to enter the land of promise to begin a new life. Moses sought to bolster their faith to enable them to live a life of obedience to God in this new land. The land of their inheritance was just ahead, but their lives there would be fraught with many dangers. Going with them was God, under whose guidance they had traveled in all their wilderness experiences, most of which had been dark and difficult.

Moses knew that the greatest threat to their future was in having no spiritual existence, and it was to this concern that he spoke. He reminded them that "The Lord their God is One." God delivered them from bondage, and gave to them the Law. Through their father Abraham, God entered into a covenant relationship with them and made them his people. God must come first with them. He required obedience, and would punish their transgressions. In this fashion they were admonished by Moses to enter their land of promise and live, individually and collectively, as people of the Living God.

This message of Moses was addressed not only to his contemporaries, but also to us. He warns us of the same need for spiritual faithfulness. These are spiritual truths that God's people of every age must embrace. God requires us to believe what he has done for us, and through our faith, to live as his people. He has led us also through many difficult problem areas of our existence, and he continues to require the same commitment of faith that Moses outlined so long ago.

A young Army wife at Fort Bragg, North Carolina, watched a former Liberian missionary give endless hours assisting military families with their problems. Soon the Army wife was coming regularly to services at the church and witnessing to others. "If Christianity can make anyone live as unselfishly as she does," the young lady said, "it must be the right way to life. If it had not been for her, I would still be searching for something to live for."

Think of the influence you have each day on those around you. What kind of witness are you for Christ and his kingdom? Does your example make others want to love the Lord and follow his way? Imagine how it would be if all Christians would truly dedicate themselves to their faith in God. The world has not yet seen what would happen if the army of the Lord really started marching!

Our technological age, with its advancing electronics and computerization, brings with it a different set of problems just as insidious as those faced by the contemporaries of Moses. Automation has led to unemployment; impersonalization of life and obsolescence of talents has led to a decline in income; audio and video technologies pervade almost every space in our lives; many rock videos promote rudeness and excesses. The list goes on and on. We need to ask ourselves some questions about our ultimate loyalties. Where is our basic faith? What is our ultimate conviction? There *are* things that one must believe — a faith to which one must hold — or else one will forever be . . . a pagan.

"Love the Lord, all you his saints! The Lord preserves the faithful!" Thus exclaims the psalmist in Psalm 31. But we must be found faithful! There is a beautiful spot for a rustic retreat in the mountains of Western North Carolina near Bat Cave. Some years ago an attractive log cabin was built there, but for some reason it was never occupied. There it stood for many years — a beautiful mountain lodge by the side of the road, well-built and ready for use — but it remained empty.

Many lives are like that mountain cabin! We dream fine dreams, yet we fail to follow through. Our lives remain empty and useless, while all about us are cries for useful, happy, and productive lives. We must be dedicated to God and filled with a vital faith to live by! And our text from Deuteronomy 4 helps us identify the essentials of that faith.

Moses tells us that first we must believe in God. Unless we are committed to him in faith we cannot please him. We must acknowledge that we are the company of people who bear his name. We must believe that God has acted to make us his very own people. According to his plan, Jesus Christ, his Son, came into our world to offer himself on the Cross in atonement for our sins, and to offer all believers the gift of eternal salvation. We must believe that the Holy Spirit has worked through the Word to bring us to faith, and that through baptism she has bound us forever to be her very own. God has done it all! It is ours, therefore, to accept his gift and to believe. For, "The Lord is God in heaven above and on the earth beneath; there is no other."

The latter part of our text admonishes us, "Therefore you shall keep his statutes and his commandments, which I command you this day, that it may go well with you, and with your children after you." Surely Moses was speaking here of faithfulness and commitment to the Law of God. He had been God's ambassador in bringing the Law to the people of Israel, and Moses commands God's people, of that time and of ours, "You shall keep His Law . . . His Statutes . . . His Commandments."

Today we have a more explicit imperative from the Gospel that is appointed for this Trinity Sunday. It is the command of our Lord, "Go therefore and make disciples of all nations, baptizing them in the name of the Father and of the Son and of the Holy Spirit, teaching them to observe all that I have commanded you; and lo, I am with you always, to the close of the age." (Matthew 28:19, 20) Jesus commands that we not simply believe, but that we also proclaim our faith in the Triune God.

There is a place just off the Blue Ridge Parkway near the Virginia-North Carolina line where the hills were blackened as far as the eye could see. A forest fire had swept the area and destroyed countless acres of forestland. One could hardly drive through the area without wondering, "What do you suppose started that terrible fire?" And we remember the repeated warnings we know so well — a single match, carelessly discarded, can start a forest fire.

Sometimes we look at our lives and say, "My life doesn't count for much." Then we remember the single match that wiped out a vast area of mountain beauty and valuable timberland. A Christian witness of "one match power" could be the influence that would set in motion a blaze of glory, proclaiming faith in the God of Creation who brought forth the beautiful mountain woodlands. The most influential pulpits of America are your desk, your workbench, your classroom. Wherever we work, there is our pulpit, and we must proclaim and give witness to our faith! This we must do to obey the command of our Lord. We must go . . . and make disciples . . . baptizing them in the name of the Father, Son, Holy Spirit. Note that Jesus refers to three persons, yet he uses the singular word "name," indicating the oneness of the three-person-God, the object of our faith.

Moses says, "The Lord is God in heaven and on earth beneath; there is no other." Jesus, in the New Testament, points to baptism in the name of the Triune God and teaches that salvation is in him alone. He commands all people to be baptized in the name of the God of the Trinity. This is where we are to begin in keeping his commandments; here is the doctrine of the Trinity in a nutshell. And as you keep this divine imperative, you are assured that "it will go well with you and with your children after you."

So ask yourself, "Is this Triune God my God? Do I behold in him the Lord who is God in heaven above and on the earth beneath?" And ask also, "Have I been baptized in his Name as Jesus requires in Matthew 28:19?" If so then you are a child of God the Father, Son, and Holy Spirit.

Remember this fact also: We must all meet this great God again — every one of us. There are no exceptions. So we must ask ourselves, are we really ready to live with him . . . in his promised Paradise? Does my manner of living, day-by-day, give evidence of my faith in his person and his name?

It has been asked, "If you were hailed into a court of law today and charged with being a believer in Almighty God, would there be enough evidence to convict you?" If so, and your ultimate faith is in him — and is evidenced in your baptism — then you are ready to meet him face-to-face. And you are joined with a host of the faithful of every age who "Know that the Lord is God; there is no other," and who are prepared, they and their children, to live with him in time and in eternity.

I think of a blind songwriter named Matheson, whose heart was broken because he was rejected in love. All circumstances of his life seemed to have been turned against him. Should he simply "curse God and die," as Job was advised? No. Instead he wrote a hymn that will always be remembered, addressed to God, entitled "O Love That Wilt Not Let Me Go." His faith is the type to which we must all aspire, the way of joy and happiness. It makes life more wonderful . . . the longer we live it.

Genesis 12:1-9   Proper 4

A Faith-Life To Emulate
John W. Cobb

The Christian's story really does not begin with the saga of Abraham. Remember, Jesus said, "Before Abraham was I am." Yet, as a practical matter Chapter 12 of Genesis is about the first episode that can be dated with fair accuracy and so may be considered a "beginning" that would cause this name to be remembered henceforth as "father of the faithful." In recent years genealogical studies have become very popular. Some from very noble motives, others merely as an expression of family pride or an ego trip. According to both Matthew and Luke Jesus' progenitors in the flesh included Abraham, son of Terah. We may be grateful that there were those in ancient times who were concerned to write down such information. Yet, even though Jesus must have been aware of his own lineage, there was something of greater importance. In his controversy with the sons of Abraham Jesus affirmed "Your father Abraham rejoiced to see my day. He saw it and was glad." (John 8:56)

Let us examine some of the qualities of Abraham in order to try to understand his place in salvation history.

Abraham was decisive. Scripture does not reveal to us the circumstances surrounding the cause of the migration of Terah's family from Ur of the Chaldees toward Canaan but for some reason the caravan stopped at Haran, remaining there until the death of Terah. Did the patriarch become ill? Was there need for a period of organization? For whatever cause the caravan halted. The father died. Now, a decision had to be made, as is so many times the need in the family upon the death of the father. And Abraham, perhaps being the oldest of Terah's three sons, would be the one to decide what to do.

Let us imagine some of the elements that went into the making of the decision to proceed. First, Abraham was a son whose early experiences included sharing life with a father who as an old man had a vision. The destiny of his descendants would be in another land. For whatever reason Terah was willing to leave the place the world knew as the "fertile crescent" to journey into the unknown.

This quotation of King George V of England, made in his 1939 Christmas message to his people during the darkest days of World War II, seems to express the spirit that motivated Terah and was likely caught and shared by his eldest son.

> *I said to the man who stood at the gate of the year "give me a light that I may tread safely into the unknown." But the man replied, "Go out into the darkness and put your hand into the hand of God. That will be for you better than light and safer than a known way."*

And so after Terah died, Abraham, who shared his father's vision, decided to press on to Canaan, meanwhile confronting the overwhelming logistics of moving a large caravan of family and animals into a new and possibly hostile environment. This was no mere emotional response to God's command. It also involved both intellect and will, the response of his whole being. There are those who would have us see in this story merely a record of one of the migrations of peoples in that area of the world, but for the faithful there is more beginning with the obedience of the spiritual father of a people.

Abraham was obedient. God spoke the word "go" and Abraham "went." For Abraham it could not have been easy to obey. He left the safety of the community he knew. He faced the task of packing and moving a herd of sheep and cattle, of caring for wives and nephews and many others. This seems so simple, and yet one knows that obedience to God's commands required much more. A prior relationship must have been established. Abraham must have recognized the one giving the order. He must have been willing to put aside personal considerations for the sake of a larger cause, acknowledging that God was in charge. And ultimately he needed the will to carry out God's command even in the face of the unknown. It was the same spirit that prompted the Apostle Paul to say: "I was not disobedient to the heavenly vision." (Acts 26:19)

Abraham was trusting. The element of trust is vital to the life of faith. It goes far beyond the mere intellectual assent suggested in the term "belief." Paul says it well: "Abraham believed God and it was counted to him for righteousness. And these words 'counted to him' have not been written for him alone but for us as well; faith will be counted to us as we believe in him who raised our Lord from the dead." (Romans 4:23-24) It is only a short step from obedience-in-trust to the response of God's people in Christ. "If you are Christ's then you are Abraham's seed." (Galatians 3:29) One can recite his creed a thousand times, but if it does not become trust and obedience then one has not found faith. With such trust there is always the ethical responsibility demanded. Later in the Genesis story God says: "I have taken care of him on purpose that he may charge his sons and family after him to conform to the way of the Lord and to do what is right and just; thus I shall fulfill all that I have promised for him." (Genesis 18:19-20)

Abraham worshiped. It may seem a minor detail that the story of Abraham includes various references "And Abraham built an altar there" at Shechem, at Bethel, at Hebron. The concomitant of obedience and trust is worship — always. How can one possibly acknowledge the God-man relationship with the expression of awe primarily in the act of worship? Perhaps this becomes the acid test of religious life today. The most recent estimates among the so-called "moderate Protestants" in America indicate that only forty-one percent of those professing church affiliation are regular attendants at worship.

Another twenty-three percent worship "occasionally" and thirty-five percent are simply "nominal" members, that is "seldom worship in the company of fellow-believers." Little wonder then that worship, primitive though it may have been, was a vital part of Abraham and his tribe.

Abraham was rewarded. This is the concept suggested in the term "blessed." "All the families on earth will pray to be blessed as you are blessed." (Genesis 12:3) Abraham's reward involved a divine relationship. As Hebrews 11:16b has it "God is not ashamed to be called their God; for he has a city ready for them." Abraham's blessedness involved a sense of his own self-sufficiency, because he depended on God and the deep knowledge that his own blessedness was to become a blessing to the whole earth.

And so for us, heirs also of the promises of God, we believe the everlasting covenant has found fulfillment in the person of Jesus Christ, a son of the tree of Abraham. Paul says it well: "If you are Christ's then you are Abraham's seed." What a glorious inheritance! What a faith-life to emulate! How much we owe to the covenant and obedience of a lonely man of long ago that we know who God is!

Genesis 22:1-18   *Proper 5*

But Where Is the Lamb?
John W. Cobb

As one stands to the West of the temple area in the old city of Jerusalem and gazes upon the remains of the Temple of Herod now spoken of as the "wailing wall," then looks beyond to the domineering Dome of the Rock, it is to recall the great epochs of history and tradition associated with the place called "Mount Moriah." How much of human history and the traditions of the "people of God" is linked to that spot!

One of the most moving and poignant of those traditions is the story of Abraham's ultimate temptation recorded in Genesis 22.

The heart of the story for us today is to be found in the question of Isaac. "And Isaac said to his father . . . Behold the fire and wood, but where is the lamb?" (Genesis 22:7b, 8) Then comes the insightful answer of Abraham, "God will provide himself a lamb for the burnt offering, my son." (Genesis 22:8) Is there a parent on earth who cannot be emotionally touched by the high drama of the father-son relationship depicted here? Abraham's obedience-in-trust had already been tested many times, but the ultimate test of faith for Abraham involved the power of human love as it is challenged by the necessity for obedience to the word of God.

The most severe temptation in life is the temptation to refuse to obey the Word and command of God — and this was Abraham's test.

In the Old Testament this temptation is hinted at many times in the challenge of God: "Prove me and try me" "Cast thy bread upon the waters and it will return unto thee after many days." And in the New Testament:

"Believe and thou shalt be saved" "I will give you another comforter. He will lead you into all truth."

The ultimate climax of the Genesis story is to be found, not in the God-arranged sparing of Isaac, but in the assurance that God would remain true to his promise that in Abraham would all the nations of the earth be blessed. Isaac would be spared to be the descendant through whom that would be accomplished. And so, one more important episode was added to Abraham's saga leading him to be known henceforth as the father of the trusting.

When Abraham answers Isaac's question with the simple statement "God will provide," one may properly question whether this was simply a "put off" by a father who wished to save his son from the agonizing truth or whether it was an expression of deep insight into the ways of God and therefore prophetic of things to come. Was Abraham's merely a blind faith or was it a faith that had already been tested and found vital? There is no way for us to know the answer. But this we can know: this was Abraham's most severe test because of the *greatness of the sacrifice*.

Unless a sacrifice is costly, it is really no sacrifice.

We are reminded of another Old Testament passage with a setting on this same hill at another much later time. When King David felt the need to make amends for his lack of trust in God by ordering a census in order to ascertain the strength of his fighting force, he went to a Jebusite named Araunah requesting permission to use his threshing-floor as the locus of sacrificial offering. Araunah, feeling honored to have such a request from so important a personage as David, quickly offered to let him use the threshing-floor and wanted to furnish him with the animal for sacrifice as well. But David replied to this offer with the penetrating response, "How can I offer to the Lord that which costeth me nothing?" (2 Samuel 24:24) Abraham's intended sacrifice would be costly to him. As so often happens, God's promises and God's commands appear to be in conflict. It is as if Abraham were saying "If I am commanded to slay my only son, how will your promise be fulfilled that in my seed shall all the nations of the earth be blessed?" Three days Abraham had to ponder this matter. His mind-set must have been very like that of Philip at the feeding of the five thousand, "We'll have people sit down and distribute the food, but we just don't believe it can happen." With this Abraham plodded on up the mountain with the fire and the wood and his only son . . . and God did provide the lamb . . . not only in the Old Testament story, but ultimately in the sacrifice of his only-begotten Son. In Christ many of the requirements of Old Testament sacrifice were met. An only son, without blemish, in prime of life, no broken bones, all the necessary requirements were there in the person of Jesus Christ.

When the congregation of Holy Trinity, Raleigh, North Carolina, was building a new house of worship, there was a conscious attempt to depict the several seasons of the Christian year in the faceted glass windows of the nave. They included Advent, Christmas, Epiphany, Maundy Thursday, et al. Then there was the Good Friday window with its Cross in the earth, a crown of thorns and nails dominated by somber shades of gray with splotches of red suggesting the wounds of Christ. But perhaps the most significant of all the symbolism was at the very top of the window — the hand extended downward, symbol of the presence of the Father, God, and saying to all who observe, "God's presence in the crucifixion was real." The suffering and death of his only Son cost God dearly. God did provide the lamb and John the Baptizer could point to Jesus and say "Behold the lamb of God who taketh away the sin of the world." (John 1:29) We therefore can sing at the eucharist "O Christ, Thou lamb of God that taketh away the sin of the world, have mercy on us."

In the celebration of the eucharist the lamb is here for us just as the lamb caught in the thicket of the mountain was there for Isaac. John, the theologian, expresses it well, "These are they that have come out of great tribulation and have washed their robes and made them white in the blood of the lamb." (Revelation 7:14)

The chief thought throughout the New Testament is the spiritual yielding of life. St. Paul caught the message when he said to the Roman Christians after an excursus on the meaning of Christ's life and death and resurrection: "I beseech you therefore . . . present your bodies a living sacrifice, holy and acceptable to God which is your spiritual service." (Romans 12:1) Not the taking of life but the giving of it, that is true sacrifice.

An additional and important insight is provided when John proclaims "The lamb shall be their shepherd and will guide them to springs of living water." (Revelation 7:17) He also sings "Worthy is the lamb that was slain to receive power and riches and wisdom and strength and honor and power and glory and blessing." (Revelation 5:12)

Yes, God did provide and continues to provide for us the lamb! Now, the question is: "Can it be said of us that our faith is a faith like Abraham's or like the faith of Christ, that sees beyond the contradictions of obedience over against trust to the faithfulness of the God who keeps his promises and of whom it can be said, 'God so loved the world that he gave . . .?"

"But where is the lamb?"

"God will provide."

Genesis 25:19-34   Proper 6

Some Crossroads of Family Life
W. Dexter Moser

And Isaac prayed to the Lord for his wife . . . and the Lord granted his prayer . . .
                                                    Genesis 25:2

The horn of the diesel train sounded in the distance, awakening me in the dawn of the morning. A horn blast sounded at every crossroad, louder and louder as the engine came near. Then it faded as it passed into the hills on the other side of the city. I then considered the many crossroads that I have had in my life and meditated on the meaning for that very day.

Today across this great land of ours, and other lands of the world, the family as a strong influential, happy and powerful unit seems to be reaching its crossroads at a faster pace. Therefore, each family unit needs to be alert through the entire span of life's great and exciting journey.

Only a short time ago, and while comparing the crossroads of the biblical family of Isaac and Rebekah, I decided, while glancing at our evening newspaper to thumb through its pages to see what crossroads our modern family may be facing. I selected some articles and posted them on sheets for my file. These were the ones discovered:

"Son gets four months on drug deal."
"Drought is bad or worse than '86 . . . particularly tough on farmers."

"It's a bad time when a little old lady is scared to come out on the streets," said Sgt. _____ supervisor of _____ squad. It's a bad time when children play around needles and drug dealers."
"A Vietnamese woman huddles with her children Thursday after the refugees arrived on an island off Hong Kong. The government this week announced a policy designed to stem the influx of refugees."
"Bethel Home for Children . . . was ordered closed last Friday when a judge ruled that its residents were subject to physical abuse, medical neglect and detention amounting to imprisonment."

Each of you has observed, in some way, the present crisis of our families in the neighborhoods, cities, and throughout this land.

What about the biblical family, like the one of Isaac and Rebekah, which our Lord created; out of which we have come; what were their strengths and weaknesses? Let's take a look at God's biblical family then; and reflect on its meaning for the family now. Obviously, the newspaper articles above have given us just a tiny peep into modern family crossroads.

The text of Genesis 25:19-34 gives us a look at five persons: Isaac, who was Abraham's son; Rebekah, Isaac's wife; Esau, older twin; and Jacob, the younger twin, and most important of all, the Lord. The verses tell us of the family of Isaac and Rebekah; the fact was that Rebekah had not conceived a child in their twenty years of marriage. This was of much concern for the early biblical woman, Rebekah, and of course to her husband, Isaac.

Our biblical family's attitude toward children may be viewed through the opening chapter in the Bible: "So God created man in his own image, in the image of God he created him; male and female he created them." And God blessed them, and God said to them, "Be fruitful and multiply, and fill the earth and subdue it; and have dominion . . . over every living thing that moves upon the earth . . ." (Genesis 1:27-31)

In Genesis Chapter 2:18 we read the explanation of God's reasoning "Then God said, 'It is not good that the man should be alone; I will make him a helper fit for him . . . .' " The despair of Rebekah and the disappointment of Isaac was caused by the fact that she had not been fruitful and multiplied the family with children.

They, Isaac and Rebekah, were at one of their crossroads. There was no child; what should be done? First, it is notable that this family possessed some qualities which are just as valuable in today's family:

A strong prayer life
Faith and trust in the Lord
Compassion for each family member
Impartiality toward each person
A sense of self-esteem and respect for each other
Assistance so that the child might have a meaningful vocation

Isaac, as husband, showed commendable reactions. He was sensitive to his wife's feelings; he was concerned for her because of her inability to become pregnant and therefore, multiply and help people the earth.

His first reaction was to pray to his Lord; "And Isaac prayed to the Lord for his wife . . ." Isaac, as husband, as head of the family, went directly to the source of power in their family, the Lord. Why did he go to the Lord about this? Because of his love for his wife, who was a helper fit for him, suitable to him, meant for him; he undoubtedly felt her despair, her feelings of not being a helper, fit for or suitable to the needs which are satisfied through the birth and life of children in the home. He prayed to God. He prayed for her. He prayed for them.

As it was with Rebekah and Isaac, so it was true with Sarah an Abraham; true of Hannah and Elkanah; and also of Elisabeth and Zacharias. Each woman was barren but late in life became a mother through intervention of the Lord. They gave birth chronologically to Isaac, Jacob, Samuel, and John the Baptizer. So it was that the Lord granted his (Isaac's) prayer, and Rebekah, his wife, conceived. In each case a crossroad of life was negotiated through prayer.

Shortly after the conception and during the pregnancy, another crossroad was reached, this time by Rebekah. We read, "The children struggled together within her; and she said, 'If it is thus, why do I live?' " (Genesis 25:22) This is, undoubtedly, an experience that many mothers have expressed in a similar questioning. Many, too, may feel or have felt, as she did in her apparent physical and mental desperation. Spiritually, she decided: "So she went to inquire of the Lord. And the Lord said to her,

> *'Two nations are in your womb, and two peoples, born of you shall be divided; the one shall be stronger than the other, the older shall serve the younger.'*"
>
> Genesis 25:22b-23

This crossroad Rebekah reached as the children were growing within her womb and as she reacted to the infants' movements. I wonder about the words "The children struggled together within her . . ." Why was "children," plural used rather than "child" singular? I asked a friend, the mother of twin sons. She said, "I knew there had to be twins because there was too much activity for just one child. The sense, the feeling in the womb that one pair of feet can't kick that many places, one set of hands can't cause that much action; I just knew there must be twins."

At the crossroad Rebekah, as did Isaac previously, went to her Lord for reassurance and received such reassurance. It reminds me, as a Christian, of Paul's words written to the Christians at Philippi; "The Lord is at hand. Have no anxiety about anything but in everything by prayer and supplication with thanksgiving let your request be made known unto God." (Philippians 4:6) Not only did this husband and wife pray but they prayed for faith, believing in the promised power of their God.

What about the next crossroad of this couple's life, the actual birth? "When the days to be delivered were fulfilled, behold there were twins in her womb." (Genesis 25:24) The first came forth red, all his body like a hairy mantle; so they called him Esau. Afterward his brother came forth, and his hand had taken hold of Esau's heel; so his name was called Jacob. Isaac was sixty years old when she bore them." (Genesis 25:25-26)

This birth was now another crossroad in the life of this family. Esau was so named because of his hairy body and the red complexion. Jacob was so named, many say because he was holding Esau's heel as he left the womb, Another meaning of Jacob's name is "to supplant" — take the place of — as Jacob does in the last of this text. However, the name that seems to relate to Jacob's life more clearly is the one translated to mean, "he (God) grants," or "he (God) protects." Over and over at Jacob's crossroads he seems to be protected.

So the characters of the boys were different and the parental relationships were different.

The crossroad of partiality or impartiality was a most dangerous choice. Or was it partially suggested by the Lord's foreknowledge or his predestination? All children are predestined to be God's people but have been given freedom of choice.

One feels that the Lord's words to Rebekah were never shared with Isaac, "two nations are in your womb . . . the elder shall serve the younger." However, it seems that Rebekah must have shown partiality of action if not of specific word to Jacob, the quiet one, who loved the home surroundings. The textual account tells that Isaac loved Esau because he ate of his wild game as his father had done earlier.

Isaac's and Rebekah's positive influence was reflected through the ages even to the crossroads of the New Testament early church. For example, at the healing of the lame man who clung to Peter and John . . . "And when Peter saw it he addressed the people 'Men of Israel, why do you wonder at this, or why do you stare at us, as though by our own power or piety, we have made him walk?' " "The God of Abraham and of Isaac and of Jacob, the God of our Fathers, glorified his servant Jesus . . . his name by faith in his name hath made this man strong . . ." He too is your Lord, our Lord, at every crossroad.

Then the final crossroad in this lesson occurred. "When the boys grew up . . . once when Jacob was boiling pottage, Esau came in from the field, and he was famished. And Esau said to Jacob, 'Let me eat some of that red pottage, for I am famished!' . . . Jacob said 'First sell me your birthright.' Esau said, 'I am about to die; of what use is a birthright to me?' Jacob said 'swear to me first:' so he swore to him, and sold his birthright to Jacob . . . Thus Esau despised his birthright." (Genesis 25:27-34)

Esau lost sight of the long-term goals of life under the pressure of present pressing physical needs. He gave up the lasting values to satisfy the present posing need. He traded off a kind of family last will and testament promised to the older son — for a bowl of stew.

We cannot walk away from our crossroads of life, but we can face them courageously through prayer, faith, compassion, impartial love of our fellow human beings, and personal esteem. Always walking in the strength of the God of Abraham, Isaac, and Jacob we find our way in his Son, Jesus Christ, who said, "I am the Way, the Truth, and the Life."

Genesis 27:10-17 — Proper 7

Jacob's Dream — A Dream Come True
W. Dexter Moser

> *Taking one of the stones of the place, he put it under his head and lay down in that place to sleep. And he dreamed . . .*
>
> Genesis 28:11-12

Jacob, with much patience, after many years finally married Rachel. In their nomadic life as shepherds, they, Jacob and Rachel, could have understood a song we sang around the campfire during a summer gathering at Lutheridge.

I had a dream dear,
you had one too
mine was the best dream
I ever knew;
Come, sweetheart, tell me
now is the time
You tell me your dream
and I will tell you mine.

What patience it would take to reach that experience. The story begins years earlier, many, many years.

There he was, Jacob, son of Isaac; Jacob, the grandson of Abraham; Jacob, the future father of twelve sons, the twelve sons whose names would become the names of the twelve tribes of the nation of Israel. Jacob was the one about whom you would say, "I never thought he'd be a preacher."

"Jacob as a single man, had left his home, Beersheba, and went toward Haran . . ." the homeland of his mother Rebekah and his grandfather, Abraham. At Rebekah's clever suggestion to her husband, Jacob had been sent to his mother's homeland to search for a wife from the family of her brother, Laban.

After a few days' journey, he arrived at "a certain place" a place believed to be in the vicinity of the location where his grandfather, Abraham, had received the promise from God. As Jacob made ready to stay there that night, he chose a stone for his pillow and stretched out for the night's rest. Undoubtedly, his mind was whirling again and again with the reasons for leaving his home. He did not know that he would not see his mother again.

He would recall so many times the recent events that were inevitably etched into his memory. Impressed within him as clearly as if it were yesterday, he could almost hear his mother's words:

> *"your brother, Esau, comforts himself by planning to kill you. Now my son, obey my voice, arise, flee to Laban, my brother in Haran, and stay with him awhile until your brother's anger turns away and he forgets what you have done to him; then I will send and fetch you from there. Why should I be bereft of both of you in one day? . . . I am weary of my life because of the Hittite women. If Jacob marries one of the Hittite women such as these,* [Esau in spite to his parents married two] *one of the women of the land, what good will my life be to me?" They, the Hittite women, had made life bitter for Isaac and Rebekah.*
>
> (Genesis 26:34)

Jacob's mind reeled and flashed, and another vision out of his memory came to mind as he shifted his position on the firm ground at Bethel as the rock pillow remained in place.

It would be most difficult for anyone of us to erase the memory of the real struggle he seemed to have with his mother, prior to Isaac's blessing being given to him. After hearing Rebekah's plea to send him off to Uncle Laban, he probably wondered, "can I ever be forgiven for one of my deeds to Esau, much less the two deeds, even though the first was many years past?" A wry flicker of a smile may have flashed across his face as he recalled Esau's hunger for the soup bowl of lentils following his hunting trip and his vow to give Jacob the two-thirds of the birthright (given to the older son) to go with Jacob's one-third for the younger. However, the memory of Rebekah's recent conversation was flooding his conscious mind. Why did he do what he did to his father and his brother?

It's hard to believe this would happen to their home. "Now Rebekah was listening when Isaac spoke to Esau. So when Esau went to the field to hunt for game and bring it . . ." (Genesis 27:5) Isaac was sure death was near and Esau agreed to fix the final ceremonial meal before getting from Isaac the final family blessing.

Rebekah probably recalled the words of some forty years earlier in her life, those during the pregnancy. It was in her late months as the twins moved violently in her womb, so much so that she went to the Lord for help. His words were as clear as if it were yesterday:

> "Two nations are in your womb, and two peoples born of you shall be divided; the one shall be stronger than the other, the elder shall serve the younger."
> (Genesis 25:23)

At this point, Rebekah, hearing that both Isaac and Esau felt Isaac would die, decided that she could not wait for the Lord, but must act for him; or her favorite son would lose the blessing. Could it possibly be that the Lord was using her vision of what she thought he meant? Was she impatient in her desire for this son?

You and I can recall the later words of Isaiah which she, of course, did not know:

> *"For my thoughts are not your thoughts neither are your ways my ways says the Lord. For as the heavens are higher than the earth, so are my ways higher than your ways and my thoughts than your thoughts."*
> (Isaiah 55:8-9)

We certainly hope that God works through us! That we this day would learn his ways and live in and by those ways! However, Jacob's hands folded under his head as the sun's rays faded. His recall of his deeds that day continued.

The words of his mother, Rebekah, flashed again:

> *"I heard your father speak to your brother, Esau. Bring me game and prepare for me savory food, that I may eat it, and bless you before the Lord before I die. Now, my son, obey my word as I command you . . .*
> (Genesis 27:6)

She gave him orders to get a choice lamb. She would fix it as Isaac liked it. She ordered him to get Esau's best coat to wear. Jacob replied, "Behold my brother Esau is a hairy man, and I am a smooth man. Perhaps my father will feel me, and I shall seem to be mocking him, and bring a curse upon me and not a blessing." (Genesis 27:11-12) She had the answers to all objections and gave them sharply and quickly. The hairy skin of the lamb would be placed on exposed places of Jacob's body; the coat of Esau was worn; the soup was given to Isaac. Isaac questioned, Jacob lied. The blessing was given and could not be recalled. Jacob had to run from Esau and his home at Beersheba to save his life.

There he was at Bethel in the open, remembering. There under the heavens all of these deeds flashed before him as he rested. Was it possible that he would never go home again?

Yet he again recalled when "Esau discovered the truth of the way Jacob had gotten the blessing." He shouted those words of Esau, which were told him.

"He took away my birthright and behold now he take away my blessing." (Genesis 27:36) And he (Jacob) knew that, ". . . Esau hated Jacob because of the blessing with which the father had blessed him and Esau said to himself, 'The days of mourning for my father are approaching, then I will kill my brother. But the words of Esau . . . were told to Rebekah." (Genesis 27:41ff)

As he lay, head on the rock in the *"certain place,"* in the limestone hill country, he finally slept.

And he dreamed that there was a ladder set up on the earth, and the top of it reached to heaven; and behold the angels of God were ascending and descending on it! And behold the Lord stood above it . . .

(Genesis 28:12-13a)

Jacob was seeing ascending angels from down where he was to above where the Lord was. He saw descending angels coming from up where God was down to where he was. This seems to show God's willingness to communicate with Jacob, his willingness to come to his created persons, those like Jacob, those like you and me, all of his children.

Some translators use words about the Lord's position as our verse says: ". . . and behold the Lord stood above it . . ." Other translators say: "stood beside him." "Stood with him."

We look up to God in reverence. He stands beside us in support. We stand with him in faith. He continually sends to us, comes to us in loving grace, always giving, giving, and giving!

His giving is never more evident than in and through his Word, awe inspiring, spoken, remembered.

". . . And the Lord (whatever his position) stood above it and said, 'I am the Lord, the God of Abraham your father and the God of Isaac' . . ." (Genesis 28:13)

One could put a comma after "I am," and, "the Lord," and see the eternal personality of God which would be indicated as Moses heard the Lord speaking at the burning bush when the Lord says, "I Am the I Am." Jacob, the quiet man who loves the tents of the family is envisioning a new family, reaching back through the ages to our creator and looking ahead to our present Christian family.

The word of promise for Jacob continues:

> . . . *the land on which you lie I will give to you and to your descendants, and your descendants shall be like the dust of the earth, and you shall spread abroad to the west and the east and to the north and to the south; and by you and all your descendants shall all the families of the earth bless themselves . . .*
>
> (Genesis 28:13-14)

Here we have the undeserved gift of God to all people, the four corners of the earth, all points of the compass, even from the rising to the setting of the sun, even to such a rascal as Jacob. Therefore, he, Jacob, is recipient of the promise and becomes one of those in that oft-repeated affirmation later spoken by the Apostle Peter: "The God of Abraham and of Isaac and of Jacob, the God of our fathers, glorified his servant Jesus . . ." (Acts 3:13a)

We bless ourselves right through to the early church and beyond. This we share through his kingdom, his servant, Jesus; through faith in him.

The word from the ladder continues as the Lord says, "Behold I am with you and will keep you wherever you go, and will bring you back to this land; for I will not leave you until I have done that of which I have spoken to you . . ." (Genesis 28)

This promise of his continued presence will continue down through and to the yet to come children of God's creation.

This reminds us immediately of, ". . . and lo I am with you always to the close of the age. (Matthew 28:20a)

This is our power for his mission to us as human grains of dust. The echo is heard in the symphonic, spiritual ring of the word, "Come O blessed of my father, inherit the kingdom prepared for you from the foundation of the world . . . Truly I say to you as you did it to one of the least of these my brethren you did it to me . . ." (Matthew 25:34, 40)

Jacob was dreaming and began to awake and as he did, he said, "Surely the Lord is in this place, and I did not know it."

God does surprise us and we too can respond with the joy of Jacob. It is through the *Word* of God that we *know* him and his way.

"And he (Jacob) was afraid . . ." and with Jacob's quietness, his reverence, his assurance he said; "How awesome is this place!" A place to remember for all time. ". . . This is none other than the house of God, and this is the gate of heaven." (Genesis 28:17)

Jacob could have affirmed the prophets future word: "Seek the Lord while he may be found, call upon him while he is near and let the wicked forsake his way, and the unrighteous man his thoughts." (Isaiah 55:6)

So Jacob could have sat up, at Bethel rubbed his eyes once more, and turned his mind toward the magnificant dream and said, "I'm sorry, forgive me." He could have repeated a very simple blessing (one used often by our Cobb forefather, the Rev. W. G. Cobb):

*Thank you Lord for the rest of last night
and for this light of a new day."* Amen

Now the imperative of the campfire song takes on new meaning;

"You tell me your dream and I will tell you mine."

Yes, go therefore and teach — go tell your dream; you are God's person. Go! God's Kingdom waits.

Tell your dream — your call from our Lord.

Genesis 32:22-32 *Proper 8*

Where Does One Go When Darkness Floods One's Life?
James K. Cobb

There are many places in the providence of God where he waits to meet with us. But there is one strange place where he can always be found. The Psalmist has described the place as the place called wits-end. In the 107th Psalm, verse 28 the Psalmist declares, "They are at their wits-end then they cry to God in their trouble." The place called wits-end is the place of our frustrations and despair. It is the place where we come to the end of our strength and wisdom and are thereby brought to that humility and helplessness by which the soul is laid open to God.

An aged Christian said recently, "Each of us must learn to face the dark moments in life alone, on our own; no one can take away or relieve some kinds of pain we have." I suggest that communion with God can help. Abraham faced the pain of sacrificing his only son; he was alone and it was dark. Jacob wrestled with an angel; he was alone and it was dark. Joseph had to pretend he didn't even know his brothers in time of hunger; he was alone and it was dark. Moses led his people to, but could not go into, the promised land; he was alone and it was dark. Peter, after living with Jesus for three years, denied him three times; he was alone and it was dark. Saul tried desperately to destroy all Christians and, walking toward

Jerusalem, heard the Lord speak; he was alone and it was dark. Jesus during temptation standing before Pilate, praying in the Garden of Gethsemane, carrying a Cross, agonizing on a Cross, being raised from the dead, was utterly alone and it was dark.

So you see there is much precedent in sacred Scripture to tell us what can happen when life tumbles in. We cannot avoid or evade fear or loneliness, or suffering or pain or death. But we can examine it, explore it, expose it, experiment with it, expect it, turn it into creative fruitful time and an experience of solitude and growth in the kingdom of grace.

The text records a providential meeting between God and man and suggests the basic truth that man's extremity is God's opportunity. Listen to the way the Bible records it: "And Jacob was left alone and a man wrestled with him until the breaking of the day . . . so Jacob called the name of the place Peniel saying, 'For I have seen God face-to-face, and yet my life is preserved.' "

Look first at the background of our text. Abraham had been called by God to be the father of Israel, the chosen nation. Abraham was faithful to his call and his son Isaac continued the heritage with courage and faith. A family was born to Rebekah and Isaac among whom were the twins Jacob and Esau. Esau the first born inherited the birthright according to the law of the tribe; but Jacob tricked his brother out of the inheritance. Naturally jealousy and bitterness caused Jacob to leave home and seek a life apart. Years passed and Jacob was married and had amassed a great fortune. Now, as the scene of our text occurs, Jacob is on his way back to the parental home, carrying a terrific burden of sin and guilt. As he approaches his destination he sends gifts to his brother to assuage that guilt. Then he divides his family and followers and sends them in different directions, so that if one is destroyed the other will be safe. Now he is utterly alone and it is in this extremity that God comes to him in the form of an angel and the wrestling takes place.

Note also that this meeting with God is extremely important; it tells us that God loves us, every one, as if there were only one of us to love. God created us and he is all-powerful. We need to be constantly reminded of the greatness of God, and, even though we are small insignificant individuals among billions of people who inhabit the earth, we are within the love and mercy of God.

Several years ago while vacationing at the beach with our family, I began my early morning walk long before the others had awakened. Each morning walk along the expansive ocean afforded time for lengthy meditation and gratitude for the glory and grace of God. Far too often we forget how powerful our creator God actually is. Yet he owns the mighty ocean and forests and fields, and never a cloud in the sky moves without his knowledge. Just so the text reveals that before Jacob was aware of his need God came to him. That still is abundantly true to this very day. Sometimes we carelessly relegate God to the backgrounds of our lives, wanting him there in case of an emergency but quite sure we can handle things very efficiently in our own way.

I remember counseling a young couple prior to their marriage; during the conversation I told them I would always be available to them if problems arose. But then the groom-to-be said, "I don't think we need the church just now, but if we do we'll come back to see you." How utterly tragic to see young people completely oblivious to their need for God and his undershepherd, not only at the beginning of their marriage but to the end of their lives. Yet the tragic truth is that there are many who feel that way. Maybe not with such brashness, but just as real a rejection nevertheless. It would seem that the best thing to do is to shrug off such attitudes, and yet God is a God of patience. He is a God of grace, so he is there, where we are, calling us even when we are not aware of it. The Apostle Paul had a word for it. "God is in Christ reconciling the world unto himself. Yet while we were yet sinners Christ died for us." That means that God is seeking you, too. The message of the Cross of Christ etches that truth for all to see in terms that can never be forgotten.

We ought also to be astute enough to know that God is interested in us enough to wrestle with us. Not because he is interested in having a battle, but in order to confront us with divine truth as we know it in Jesus Christ. Christ had little patience with those who wished to argue religion, but he had great patience with honest doubters, people with questioning minds. His purpose was and is to confront us with the truth about God and to challenge us to the Christian way of life.

Second we must be sincere in our struggles with God. We cannot dismiss God by calling him the man upstairs who seems to be in the shadows keeping watch above his own. He will be willing to help, but we must be sincere about what he says and wants us to do and to be. We sometimes believe we can relegate God to the sidelines of our lives by keeping inviolate the separation of church and state. I have some problems with the fearful fetish developing in the framework of separation, where we leave the impression with our school children either that God does not exist or that we must not talk about him in school — not even answer the natural questions which a child's mind normally poses.

We must be concerned that the education of our children include recognition of the reality stated by the supreme court as, "We are a religious people whose institutions presuppose a supreme being," and that this is an implicit assumption without sectarian divisiveness. Our children and we ourselves need to be aware of the important role religion has always played in history and in our American culture.

Jacob had been trying to run away from God. Now facing one of the crises of life, he became frantically aware of the fact that life couldn't go on that way. He learned as you and I must eventually learn that life without God is no life at all. Only the fool hath said in his heart there is no God, and only a fool attempts to live his life apart from God. In every road Jacob traveled he came again to a roadblock. Finally, he knew that he would have to face the person he had wronged. Christ has said it this way: If your brother has something against you, not if you have something against him, set it straight then come and offer your gift to God. You see it works both ways. Relationships with God are dependent on your attitudes and relations with your fellowpeople. These facts demand that we be sincere on our meetings with God.

Good intentions often give way to dismal failure. The road to hell is paved with good intentions; no matter how sincere they are, good intentions are not enough when it comes to your dealings with God. That means that we must be tenacious in our wrestling with God.

We must stay our course in our relationships with God. Jacob was tenacious in his relationship with God. When you are concerned about your soul salvation, cling to God. God alone is dependable; therefore cling to him. Even when your own conscience accuses you or the voice of Satan would come to disturb your fellowship with God, cling to God, he will never let you go. Your sins may seem like a nightmare and you may be tempted to yield to despair; but trust alone in God.

Finally God will bless you where you are. Is that possible? Not only is it possible but it is God's glorious promise. Listen to God's invitation. "Turn to me and be saved." Go then and share this blessing with others. Tell others of God's grace to you in Christ. Remember that even through the bitter darkness, the anguish of pain and suffering, paint your life with shadows. God can bless you there. Wasn't that Jacob's experience? It wasn't easy to cross the brook to meet his brother. It wasn't pleasant to face truth and admit his sins in his relation with his brother or others; so he had to wrestle with God at this point, and that is precisely where God blessed him. What then is the rest of the story? It means to take the worst that life can do to you or the worst you can do to yourself and turn it into victory at the Cross. The Cross at Calvary shows **you how.**

Exodus 1:6-14, 22:2-10   Proper 9

Expectations of a Vital Faith
James K. Cobb

The lessons appointed for the ninth Sunday after Pentecost reflect on the issue of the power and presence of God in the context of suffering. This narrative gives us no easy answers. If anything they exclude some cherished complacencies such as belief that God protects his people from suffering and pain and anguish and hopelessness. But in the text, suffering is undeserved and prolonged and bitter. The fact is that ordinary people lose control of their lives and see their children abused and murdered; but just as complacency is denied in this text, so is the complacency of despair. The people do not give up, instead they resist the cruelty of Pharaoh.

So you see that the perplexities of faith are as old as religion itself. There is a stage when belief in God raises problems instead of solving them. This is particularly true in the experience of one of the Old Testament stalwarts by the name of Gideon. His people had been for seven years in a desperate situation. The enemy had driven them into the hills where they had to grow and thresh their corn in secret places to keep it from falling into the hands of the bandits. It is all quite familiar and characteristic of those who feel insulated from suffering because they are God's people. When the messenger of God came to him and saluted him with the words from Judges 6:13, "And Gideon said unto him, Oh my Lord, if the Lord be with us, why then has all this befallen us?" His immediate reply seems a bit contemptuous. "The Lord be with us," he said in effect. I don't see much sign of that. If the Lord be with us, why then has all this befallen us?

That's precisely the implied question answered by a theologian who wrote recently: "It is our Christian privilege to communicate to our children a faith which will stand in the midst of unsolved riddles of life with an undaunted hopefulness. The discovery that such a faith is possible is the beginning of our real discovery of God."

How often has the cry of Gideon been heard from the depths of suffering and pain? Here is a woman whose husband has been taken in the prime of life. She just cannot understand it. It is not that she doesn't believe in God and his infinite love. It is just that she cannot fit the two together, and they do not make sense. If the Lord be with us, she says, why has this befallen me?

One hears it time and again from people who look around at the agony of our world today. The love of God seems an empty phrase amid the bursting bombs, hostility between nations, the horror of ruined cities, self pity, cruelty, and despair. If God cares about people why do so many millions starve and die? How can we square what is happening in our world today with the belief in an Almighty God and Father? The Christian creed is like a feeble lamp; it only makes the darkness darker. It does not seem to make sense. "If the Lord be with us why then does all this happen to us?"

It is useless to suggest that we have easy answers to the continuing riddle of life. But there are some things we do know, and those glorious promises and assurances of God's presence are replete in sacred Scripture. "In the beginning God"; and with that word to begin our scripture, we believe, we are assured, we expect that God was in the beginning, will be at the end, and is present in all there is in between. "The Lord is my shepherd, I have no other needs." That assurance tells us that we can always expect the presence of God to be near, to guide, to support and to protect. "The Lord will keep your going out and your coming in, now and forever." We can expect the Lord to be close at hand in all our comings and goings. In the New Testament Jesus says, "I am the alpha and the omega, the beginning and the ending, I will be with you to the end of this present age."

I tell you Christianity would be a dead faith without expectation of vital faith, if we had no hope for the present or future. Hope would be shattered, meaning would be lost, future would be empty. Whatever the situation, it is better to stand with Christ and for his way of life than to slink out of the moral struggle in cynical despair. There are some fixed stars that no darkness can drown. Whatever is unreal, some things are real and ring true. The patience, the courage, and the love that shine in Christ are real. His Cross has burned the glory of these things into the soul of the world so indelibly that nothing can ever dim them. Whatever the darkness, we can steer by these fixed stars.

But there is an answer to Gideon and to us. Part of it is the fact that suffering does not contradict the loving care of God. Some people are irritated by the statement that suffering does us good. Some may even deny it, arguing from themselves. It all depends of course on the attitude we take toward it, the mind on which it falls, and that is in our own hands. The wind that drifts one sailor on the rocks will send another on his way. It all depends on how they handle the boat.

Second, Gideon knew another part of the answer. The things that had befallen them were due to themselves. The people had fallen away from their old faith and the life it commanded. It did not mean that God had forsaken them. The Bible leaves no doubt about God's hand in the process. The Lord, it dares to say, delivered them into the hands of the Midianites. It is not because God does not love that things turn out badly. It may be even because God loves us. It is because God's love is at the basis of life and all that it offers us that life turns against us when that love is defied. Loveless and faithless living in a world built to run on the principles of love is bound to bring disaster.

Again Gideon discovered yet another answer. It was his own spirit. Where did he get the spirit that revolted against evil around him? Where did he get the spirit of resistence that made the angel call him a mighty man of valor? Surely it was because in the darkness God was with him. Have we not found the same evidence in many individual lives?

That is precisely the expectation of a vital faith in the power of God revealed so splendidly in the experience of Job. He had lost all of his possessions, he who had been the richest man in the east. Next his ten children were killed in a windstorm which hit the house where they were celebrating a birthday. Then Job himself was afflicted with the excruciating pain of an ugly skin disease. In this dilemma his wife suggested that he should forget God and take his own life. Where was his God? It was then that Job exclaimed with a triumphant faith, "though He slay me, yet will I trust him." (Job 13:15)

God's ultimate wisdom is good. Times without number Christians have been faced with hardships and trials which seemed unjust and unreasonable. In such crises believers have felt sure that the ultimate wisdom of God would turn all things to their eternal good.

As Job faced his friends who accused him of hypocrisy, he declares, "I will trust God; the Lord gave and the Lord taketh away, blessed be the name of the Lord." However, in such crises we Christians are often perplexed and often rebellious. On the one hand we are tempted to question the wisdom of God and on the other we doubt that God has the power to help us out of our specific dilemma.

Do we think God is giving us empty promises? He has told us he will never leave or forsake us. Is it wistful thinking to believe we have his everlasting arms beneath us? He promises we will never be tempted above what we are able to bear. Can we believe God? Or do we doubt that God really is? The faith that cannot be shaken is the faith that holds fast saying, "Though he slay me, yet will I trust him. I know that my redeemer liveth."

The faith that cannot be shaken is found at the Cross as the final assurance of God's love. When the home burns down and we stand over the ashes of all that we had; when the floods descend and sweep away crops before the harvest; when death comes to our home and takes from our midst our dearest child, it may seem as if God has forgotten us and even failed us. Naturally the thought comes to us. "Surely God cannot permit this to happen and still be a God of love."

In such an hour Christians come stumbling to the Cross to behold the amazing love of God who spared not his own Son but freely gave him up for us all that we might be redeemed from the curse of the Law and find heaven as our eternal home. God sent his Son into the depths of hell that you and I might be forgiven, that you and I might find the glory of heaven where there shall be no sorrow or death.

The sacrifice of Jesus proclaims the loving kindess of God and gives us the blessed assurance that God does not want us to perish but have everlasting life. Though our sins be as scarlet, though we have sinned often, in and through the atoning death of Christ we become heirs of his endless glory. Though our bodies squirm under pain, though we grow feeble and old, waste away and finally die, this corruptible body must put on incorruption and this mortal must put on immortality. Greater than any heartaches of this life is eternal separation from God in eternity. None of us need face this possibility since Jesus died for us on Calvary's Cross. With Job we can say as we rise above suffering and loss, pain and despair, "though he slay me, yet will I trust him, therefore I place my life in God's hands for time and eternity."

The hymn writer has said it best.

O for a faith that will not shrink,
Though pressed by many a foe,
That will not tremble on the brink
Of poverty or woe;
That will not murmur nor complain
Beneath the chastening rod,

*But in the hour of grief or pain
Can lean upon its God.
Lord, give me such a faith as this,
And then, whate'er may come,
I taste e'en now the hallowed bliss
Of an eternal home. Amen*
(William H. Bathurst, 1796-1877)

Exodus 2:11-22 Proper 10

A Noble Patriotism
John D. Mauney, Jr.

"The first breath of freedom stirs the air." So exclaimed President Reagan in his address to the students and faculty of Moscow State University, as he commented on his talks with Soviet Leader Mikhail Gorbachev in the Moscow Summit of June, 1988. Mr. Reagan went to Moscow as an agent of peace and a champion of human rights. The people of the U.S.S.R., who are enslaved under the Communist regime, must have the opportunity to chart their own courses in life, and Mr. Reagan envisioned himself as their ambassador of freedom in his role as a national leader.

Through the course of human history, many men and women have served in such a capacity. Corrie Ten Boom was a heroine of the anti-Nazi underground as she worked and prayed for persecuted Jews and Christians. In Civil War days, Harriet Tubman and Quaker Leader Thomas Garrett developed and labored through the "railroad to freedom," liberating thousands of slaves and religious leaders from the yoke of slavery in the old South. George Washington led the early Americans from the shackles of tyranny in their struggle for freedom. And during the Reformation, Martin Luther espoused the cause of freedom for people in spiritual bondage under ecclesiastical domination.

Thus, our text for this Sunday deals with events in the early life of Moses, as God prepared him for a unique mission to lead his Chosen People out of bondage in the land of Egypt.

Moses was a noble patriot! His greatness is acclaimed in both the Old and New Testaments, and we take special note of the statement from the Acts of the Apostles: "And Moses was instructed in all the wisdom of the Egyptians, and he was mighty in his words and deeds." (Acts 7:22)

These are the words of Stephen, who came to be recognized as a leader among the early Hebrew Christians. Envious of his wisdom and the spirit with which he spoke, opponents of the early Christians had called him before the council, charging him with blaspheming against Moses and against God. In response to the questions of the high priest, Stephen delivered an eloquent defense of his faith and actions and those of his Hebrew-Christian colleagues. He acknowledged the God of the Hebrews as his God, and Moses as God's lawmaker and faithful advocate. He tells the story of God leading his people in the days of the patriarchs, their eventual enslavement in the land of Egypt, and their worsening persecution to the point where their children were put to death. At this critical juncture Stephen introduces Moses as God's liberator of the Hebrews.

Moses was born of a Levite couple, and he was beautiful to behold! Only three months after his birth, to prevent his slaughter by the Egyptians, his mother placed him in "the basket of bulrushes," resulting in his adoption into the Pharaoh's court as the potential ruler of Egypt. "And Moses was instructed in all the wisdom of the Egyptians, and he was mighty in his words and in his deeds."

Even the supernatural works of Almighty God are performed through natural means. Miracles of healing occur through the medium of medicine; multitudes are fed using fish and barley loaves. It was necessary to train and prepare one of the enslaved people "in all the wisdom of the Egyptians," and Moses was placed in the Court of the Pharaoh to develop the qualities of character required of a divinely appointed deliverer.

Israel was a nation of nomads, well acquainted with the ways of shepherds and flocks, and was sinking fast into the degraded animalism of slavery. To free the Israelites from their bondage, it was necessary that one man should possess the culture and mental grasp required of a deliverer and lawgiver. God was working to prepare one of his noblemen for this venture requiring the unique qualities of passion and faith, and the Lord God would not call him to a mission for which he was not prepared. So Moses' instruction in the wisdom of the Egyptians continued for many years.

While he was being groomed in the Egyptian courts for the mantle of leadership, it became apparent that his kinship with his own people was somehow miraculously maintained. Some association was continued with his real Levite parents, else the qualities of Messianic hope referred to in the Book of Hebrews would not have developed. In Hebrews 11:26 we read, "Moses considered abuse suffered for the Christ greater wealth than the treasure of Egypt, for he looked to the reward."

We know that deep inside, Moses was a true Israelite willing to suffer reproach because of his faith in the coming of "the Christ" in the fullness of time, and that he believed this faith held the promise of eventual reward. Moses was, indeed, well instructed in the wisdom of the Egyptians, but through it all he retained the faith of a noble, patriotic Hebrew.

But all of this wisdom acquired through his years in the courts of Egyptian royalty did not destroy the in-bred faith of Moses. As Stephen says in Acts 7:23, when he was forty years old "it came into the heart of Moses to visit his brethren." So he went into the land of the Hebrews, and our text tells us that when "he looked on their burdens" and saw an Egyptian abusing a Hebrew, Moses smote the Egyptian and slew him.

Here was the action of a patriotic Israelite who retaliated in haste. Like most acts of passion, this was both an impulse of the moment, and an outcome of long-gathering forces. The cruel abuse of one of his own countrymen was the proverbial "straw that broke the camel's back," and Moses was willing, at this point, to risk everything to protect his enslaved "brother."

The next day, Moses saw two of his fellow Hebrews struggling, says our text, and he attempted to reason with them to resolve their anger. In describing this incident, Stephen, as recorded in Acts 7, uses the word "brethren" twice. He also tells us that Moses himself used the word in rebuking them as he said, "Men, you are brethren, why do you wrong each other?" (Acts 7:26) His patriotic fervor springs to the fore as he declares his own passion for peace among his people, and his compassion for their enslavement as an entrampled race.

Moses made the choice to put aside his disguise as an Egyptian nobleman and to cast his lot with his persecuted and maligned countrymen. It was an heroic decision, and it appears to have come about quite suddenly. But sometimes God allows the issues of a lifetime — perhaps of an eternity — to be decided by a sudden word or a hasty blow. Sometimes events occur which appear to be instantaneous, when in reality they have been "brewing" for a long time.

Recently the news media reported the explosion of a church in New York State. The boiler exploded and the empty church was destroyed as windows and doors were blasted and pews were tossed to and fro. This explosion was not caused simply by a sudden spark — there had been an accumulation of gases from a long-standing problem with a faulty heating system.

What a wonderful thing it would be to experience explosions in the people occupying church pews, rather than in the basement below. For if we open our hearts to Christ, he is able to make us new creatures; if our faith, like that of Moses, is strong enough, it can produce explosions in our lives that will yield great benefits for those around us. Witness the mistake of a bookbinder, who rebinding a worn New Testament, mistakenly labeled it TNT! Thank God that such sudden happenings do not belong only to violence.

Moses acted hastily in his zealous effort to champion the cause of his own people. Slaying an Egyptian seems an unwarranted and presumptuous act, and would carry an extremely heavy penalty. But his motives were good and his heart was true. He merely needed a discipline to prepare himself further for his mission; discipline he would develop in forty years of wilderness wanderings as he and his people remained in prolonged exile. Now we are beginning to understand something of the character of Moses, who was to become the Lawgiver of Israel. These verses illustrate his passion for justice, his impatience with wrong, his hot temper (of which there will be many examples in the future), and his prudence in avoiding unnecessary danger.

Perhaps the most influential men of the Bible are Abraham, Moses, and Paul. All three were patriotic, intellectual giants of their respective times. Each made mistakes of judgment and failed in given situations, and this was most certainly true of Moses. His action recorded in the text was too hasty, and yet was born of a noble patriotism. He was a loyal Israelite. Sometimes one acts to offer support to a country that is unworthy of support; but there exists a loftier passion which will brave estrangement and denunciation to act in opposition to that country's ills. Such was the patriotism of Moses. But he suffered for his error; realizing that his impulsive deed was known, he feared for his life, and fled into the land of Midian. And in this strange land there came to pass the later events described in our text.

Moses' interference on behalf of the daughters of the priest of Midian reflects great credit on the character of our hero. When the women came to the community well to draw water for their father's flock, the shepherds came and drove them away. But Moses arose from where he was sitting, opposed the shepherds, and assisted the young women in caring for their herds by giving them water. This was an energetic, fearless, and chivalrous act, providing yet another example of the heroic courage of our noble patriot!

When the young women returned home, they told their father of the events that occurred at the well. Immediately he sent someone to invite "the stranger" to come to their dwelling place for a meal as the guest of honor. As the result of his intervention, Moses was eventually married to one of Ruel's daughters, Zipporah. They made their home in Midian and Moses' sojourn there was to continue for many years.

Here we are offered a glimpse into the life of one of God's real heroes — the one called to be the leader and deliverer of the Chosen People of God. He was to lead the Israelites through forty years of wilderness wanderings and would ultimately bring them to safety in Canaan, the Land of Promise. But it came to pass that Moses himself was not permitted to enter that land, which was the goal of their long journey. He viewed it from afar, as we read in the final chapter of the Book of Deuteronomy, but God said to Moses, "I will give it to your descendants . . . but you shall not go over there." (Deuteronomy 34:4) "So Moses, the servant of the Lord, died there in the land of Moab, according to the Word of the Lord, and he buried him in the valley in the land of Moab opposite Bethpeor; but no man knows the place of his burial to this day." (Deuteronomy 34:5)

> *By Nebo's lonely mountain,*
>   *On this side Jordan's wave,*
> *In a vale in the land of Moab*
>   *There lies a lonely grave;*
> *And no man knows the sepulcher,*
>   *And no man saw it e'er;*
> *For the angels of God upturn'd the sod*
>   *And laid the dead man there.*
>   (Cecil Frances Alexander, "The Burial of Moses.")

That was a long time ago, and much has transpired since that day. The Messsiah has come. The long-promised Lord of Life has come into our world as the Word-made-flesh. In the fullness of time God's plan of salvation has been completed. The New Testament tells of many wonderful occurrences in the course of his coming as the Son of God to be the Savior of the world, but all these happenings came to pass many generations after the life and burial of Moses.

Although the patriotism of our Old Testament hero was not rewarded with entry into the promised land, nevertheless there is a glorious sequel recorded in Matthew 17. Moses was brought forward with the Prophet Elijah, to view a sight even more glorious than that of Canaan of old. He was privileged to stand with Jesus, the King of Salvation and Savior of the world, on the Mount of Transfiguration. He did not stand in the land of Canaan, but rather stood in full view of the Messianic Savior whose countenance shone brightly as a token of his eternal glory. And the disappointment of Moses diminished as God continued to work in mysterious ways. For you see, all things do work together for good to the people of every generation and age who truly love the Lord God.

O lonely grave in Moab's land!
O dark Bethpeor's hill!
Speak to these curious hearts of ours,
And teach them to be still.
God hath his mysteries of grace,
Ways that we cannot tell,
He hides them deep, like the hidden sleep
Of him he loved so well.
(Cecil Frances Alexander, "The Burial of Moses.")

Exodus 3:1-12   *Proper 11*[1]

Pilgrimage of Faith
John M. Cobb

To begin, let me just note that some of what follows is quoted.[2]

"In 1817 a group of 1,400 families, consisting of about 9,000 souls, set out under the leadership of [one] Johann Koch, a miller of [the town of] Schluchter in Wuerttemberg"[3] (i.e., in Southwest Germany) to emigrate to the Caucasus region of Central Russia. From studies in the Book of Daniel and the Revelation, they were convinced that somewhere there in the east, " 'near the original cradle of the human race' . . . the *Savior* would [return and] commence his personal reign."[4]

It *was* the *era* of the *Napoleonic wars* in Germany — a time economically and personally *stressful* if not disastrous; and thus many were open to the idea of *emigration*.[5]

Thus, "they looked eastward for a place of refuge, where the elect could escape from the plagues that would afflict mankind."[6]

> *Having disposed of their immovable property in their native land, they placed their families and goods on rafts and sailed down the Danube past . . . Vienna, Presburg, and Belgrade, singing Millenial hymns, until they reached the Black Sea . . . Because of epidemics and various adverse conditions unforeseen, only a few ever reached their destination — less than 100 souls.*[7]

(No, they did not all die along the way, many just dropped *out*; and, as well, others came later.)

However, those who *did* make it found Central Russia

a forbidding region of mountains and dry barren valleys . . . *[These] new villages undoubtedly experienced the most* trying *ordeals of* all *the* German settlements *in* Russia. *The climate here was hot and dry, and the soil could be made productive only by irrigation. Epidemics of fever were frequent in the early years and killed off hundreds of settlers. The neighboring Persians and Kurds often attacked the new villages, plundering, destroying and carrying off people into slavery. For many years only the fittest could survive, and the growth of the colonies remained at a standstill. The harsh conditions, however, in time* sobered up *the erstwhile religious fanatics and turned them into* exemplary Christians *who prayed and toiled to eke out an existence from the barren soil. Their industry and ingenuity eventually triumphed over the wilderness and [they]* built *oases of* prosperity *in this forbidding frontier land.*[8]

Dear friends,
 I have read the above — not especially to entertain you, nor just to show what amazing things some of our stubborn German forefathers were capable of — rather, I have read it so that we can (now) take more seriously *what is involved* — when someone thinks that God has chosen *him* to lead his people out to this or that place in the desert.
 I mean, we know *now* what *happened* as Moses obeyed the command of God to lead his people out of the trying and adverse circumstances of slavery in Egypt, *into* the *desert* and *there* — at the holy mountain — to worship him.
 But, at that time, *they didn't know* how it was all going to turn out.
 So, when you *think* about it, it is not at all *strange* to *see* this *doubt* — yes, turmoil — that Moses must go *through* if he is to agree to *lead his people*:

 'Who am I that I should go to Pharaoh, and bring the sons
 of Israel out of Egypt?'   (v. 11)

And, further, it is not really so strange to see the *doubt* and *reluctance* of the *people* back in Egypt as Moses returns and offers to lead them *from* slavery and *to* the *promised* land.
But *first*, to the holy mountain, in the desert, where they were to meet *God*.

I think, today, that this text — "the appearance of God in the burning bush" — that this text is *familiar enough*.
We are all familiar with the simple *fact* of this *miracle*. We all remember, more or less, how the people of Israel had been made *slaves* in Egypt, how they apparently had had to *work* to make those great *pyramids* that the world still admires. And we are also likely to remember the story of *Moses* and how he *got* out there *in* the desert *to* the *place* of that burning bush.

For it seems that the Egyptians had been engaging in a bit of *population* control: The Hebrews were becoming too many, so the Egyptians decided to limit them by killing their children.

They were more straightforward in their population control than some people are today — instead of covering up their population control with terms like "fetus," "right to have control over one's body," "psychological and social danger factors," *etc.*, they just took the little fellows and drowned them.

And then we remember how *Moses* was *saved* from this fate by the Egyptian *princess* who *found* him, and how he grew up — apparently with his own mother as his nurse — but with all the privileges of the Egyptian palace.

And so there you have it: Moses — by birth and tradition a member of a religious-cultural *minority* group —
"primitive" and of nomadic tradition — but by adoption and education — *Moses* — a member of the *majority* culture —
well-organized, technologically competent, but also — *Godless*. (I mean, yes, they did have their god; but it was *not* God himself, but rather their own projection.)

So Moses is there in Egypt, a part of two cultures. And it may have *seemed* as if the *Egyptian* culture had gotten the upper hand in him — for he was considered a part of the royal family, and that would mean a position in the Egyptian government.

Yet, underneath, this tension . . . the conflict — which came to the *fore* that day when he saw an Egyptian beating a Hebrew slave; and then Moses *killed* the Egyptian and had to flee — *away* — *out* into the desert, out into that area where the *nomads* roamed:
> — yes, some still practicing the religion of their *fathers*
> — *yes*, back to the place of the *God* of their fathers . . .

"[And] God called to him out of the bush, 'Moses, Moses!' . . . And he said, 'I am the God of your father, the God of Abraham, the God of Isaac, and the God of Jacob.'" (vv. 4, 6)

The story *is* a familiar one to us:
— We remember as *children* the bush that did not burn.
— We remember the call to Moses, how he didn't want to go. But how finally he *did*. (I can recall quite clearly this text being used for a sermon on the occasion of missionaries being sent to another country.)
— We remember this text for what it says about *God* — that here God reveals to his people his sacred *name*.
— And we remember — I recall specifically — how this text has been used to show clearly how *God* in the Old Testament is not just a God of *law* and *wrath* but *also* a God of *mercy*:

I have seen the affliction of my people who are in Egypt, and I have heard their cry . . .
I know their sufferings,
and I have come down to deliver them . . .
(vv. 7, 8a)

Yes, the text is familiar to us from *many* points of view.

But, today, I want to concentrate on yet *another* aspect — one which may be a bit neglected, but which, I think, is the point where many of *us* relate to this text more closely —

I mean, today, I want to try to look at this text, i.e., the event, from the point of view of the *Hebrews*, the Hebrew *slaves*, in *Egypt*:

Because, I really don't think that too many of us are *in* the position of Moses — struggling to decide on whether or not to take on a position of leadership.

There are only a *few* of us who struggle with the call to become missionaries.

Rather, it seems that many *more* of us are in the position of those Hebrew slaves in Egypt — confronted now with the question: *Whom* will you *serve*?

I remember, when I was a boy, growing up in the United States, that there was one part of this story I could *hardly understand*; and that was:

— why these slaves were so reluctant to go!

— why they *resisted* the leadership of Moses!

And *then*, once they had gotten *out into* the desert — how it was that some kept wanting to go *back*! As the saying goes "to the fleshpots of Egypt." I mean, as a good "freedom-loving" American, I just couldn't understand why *anyone* would not *do* just about *anything* to escape from slavery!

I think now, after having been in and out of a few minority situations, after learning a few things about what Christians can or cannot do in supposedly "free" societies, after seeing the tremendous propaganda effect, the *pull* of advertising, the power of the State, and the pressure of society, I think *now* it has become somewhat more clear.

Yes, and when you consider the "freedom" that those German *colonists* had to *emigrate* to Russia to wait for the Second Coming, and what then *happened* to that freedom, then you begin to look at things in a somewhat *different* light.

For it seems now that *freedom*, although important — and certainly *no* one wants to be simply a *slave* to another — although freedom *is important* — it seems that *equally* important, in this story and also for us, *is*: "But *whom* will you *serve*?"

For certainly, after the people of Israel had come *out*, they could *not* just do what they *wanted*. Just as, for us, children cannot, generally, do what *they* want, but are bound to do what the parents want. And parents cannot always do what *they* want, but must often comply with what the government wants or what "the boss" wants.

And so, yes, freedom is indeed *important*, but *equally* as important is the question: "But *whom* will *you serve*?"

And, it seems to me that many, many of these Israelites, though, not "quite content," were *still*, *more willing* to serve the *Egyptians*, and by implication *their false gods*, than to take the *risk* necessary to serve *God himself*.

Slavery is *serving* the wrong god.

And *freedom* is serving the *true* God, a God of *justice*.

For what *is* freedom, anyway? It is being *free* or *able* to *do* what you *should* do. And inner freedom is really *wanting* to do what you really should do.

That is freedom: political and economic freedom — being free and *able* to do what you should do; and *Christian* freedom, or *inner* freedom — really *wanting* to do what you should do.

I think that a lot of those Israelites did not especially like being slaves in Egypt — no doubt about it. But I think that a lot of them liked even *less* the prospect of worshiping *God* and the *risk* that *that* entailed. And so they remained slaves — until God — out of *pure grace*, for *none* of them *deserved* it — until God — with great *signs* and *wonders* brought them *out*. And *still* some of them wanted to go back: away from the freedom of God, and back to a godless society, back to the *security* of *slavery*.

Dear friends,

Where is that *security* of *slavery* in *our* lives?

I mean, yes, we do talk a lot about having *political* freedom, but *do* we in fact *serve* and *worship God* as we *ought*? Or, are we *secure*, nicely conformed to the ways of "our society," but *also enslaved* to it? You know, sometimes, especially in these matters, a person can be *enslaved* and hardly even *know* it. Sometimes the slavery is just *so comfortable* compared to risking "trouble."

So I would ask you today to *test* yourself by asking yourself a few simple questions: First, since one of the obvious features of "our society" is its *lack* of *Christian character* (I mean, when the noted historian, John Webster Grant, writes about the breakdown of Christendom in Canadian society, I don't know of anyone who can dispute him. I think we *all* agree that religion just *doesn't play* the *role* in people's *lives*, in general, that it did 100 *years* ago.), then you and I need to *ask* ourselves the *question*: How is *my* life, how are *my* goals in life, substantially *different* from those around me?

I'm afraid that for some of the Israelite slaves (although they were obviously a lower *social* class), their *goals* in life were not too much different from those of the *Egyptians*: to eat, sleep, and get that *pyramid* built — These were *slaves indeed*!

So now we must ask *our*selves: Is *our* goal mostly to eat and sleep and go to Disneyworld and help build the next skyscraper office building? *Or*, do we maybe do some of this, but *long* and *strive* after something *much different*? Do we also strive after the service and help for *other* people and not just ourselves, strive after the praise and worship of *God* and not just our*selves*?

Let me leave that thought with you for this afternoon, to carry around with you for this week; and then, let me also add the following:

How, specifically, can my life be oriented (or reoriented) to *concern* itself mostly with the *needs* of *others* and the *praise* and *worship* of *God*? Think about *that* this *week*. Carry *that* thought *with* you when you go to work in the grocery store, or the hospital, or when you make a few rounds with the haybine this week.

"*How, specifically*, can *my* life be *oriented* or *directed* to *concern* itself mostly with the *needs* of *others* and the *praise* and *worship* of *God*. . . .

God . . . has already *done everything necessary* to *save* us and make us *willing servants* of him. And he continues to *speak* to us in our daily devotions and in Bible reading to give us *ideas* on *how* to *better* serve him. Yes, he *continues* to *speak* to us. Let *us listen* to him and *claim* our freedom, no matter *what* the *risk*!

May God *bless* you and *free* you from any and all slavery! Amen

NOTES

[1] This sermon, with only slight modification, was delivered on June 26th, 1988 at Emmaus Lutheran Church, Drayton Valley, Alberta.

[2] The following quotations combine (a) a detailed account of one particular emigrating party by George Eisenach (*Pietism and the Russian German in the United States*, Berne, Indiana: The Berne Publishers, 1948, pp. 50-55) together with (b) a description of that emigration movement in general by Adam Giesinger (*From Catherine to Krushchev: The story of Russia's Germans*, Battleford, Saskatchewan: Marian Press, 1974, pp. 39-42); for, in fact, there were several parties which set out at that time to emigrate from South Germany to Russia.

The use of lengthy quotations and the device of reading the whole story (and adding comments) is there mostly for the sake of homiletic style. The emigration itself is well-known in the literature concerning Germans in Russia (Both Eisenach and Giesinger cite a variety of secondary sources); but to the average congregation in North America, even those with descendents of Russo-Germans (as is the case in Drayton Valley), the events described would appear most unusual, perhaps even bizarre.

[3] Eisenach, pp. 53-4.

[4] *Ibid.*, p. 52. Emphasis is mine.

[5] The actual emigration, of course, took place just after the Napoleonic wars, but reflects ideology generated during that period. Notable in this regard are the writings of Jung-Stilling and the influence of Madame de Kruedener, "the Lady of the Holy Alliance," who was a close friend of Tsar Alexander. (See Eisenach, pp. 51-2.)

[6] Giesinger, p. 39.

[7] Eisenach, p. 54.

[8] Giesinger, pp. 41-42. The emphases are mine.

Exodus 3:13-20

Proper 12

Remembering the Name of God
John W. Cobb

There is an ancient Jewish legend that says: A young man asked his Rabbi "Why does your daily prayer say, 'God of Abraham, God of Isaac, God of Jacob? Why does it not simply say, 'God of Abraham, Isaac, and Jacob?' " The Rabbi replied, "because, my son, Abraham's God and Isaac's God may not have been Jacob's. Each generation must find God for itself, indeed, each person must find his own God." This legend touches on the passages of our lesson from Exodus 3, but with significant differences, lessons to be learned by the Israelites as they languished in captivity, lessons to be remembered by them throughout their subsequent history.

The setting for this lesson of religious history for Israel was the sheep pasture of Midian. The human medium was the refugee Moses.

Israel's first lesson as a people in dire need is that *God takes the initiative in deliverance.* About all this enslaved people could do was to cry out for help. That they did, but otherwise the story of their misery in bondage was replete with the feeling of helplessness and hopelessness. Yet God saw and heard their groaning and therefore chose a leader for them.

Sometimes we are caught in an impossible situation in life from which we cannot extricate ourselves. All we can do is cry out. It was to such a situation that Luther spoke when he said, "Even the Christian's groan is a prayer to God." The important thing to know, however, is that God hears our groanings as St. Paul says in Romans 8:26b. "Through our inarticulate groanings the Spirit himself is pleading for us, and God who searches our inmost being knows what the Spirit means, because he pleads for God's people in God's own way." (NEB)

God's initiative for man's deliverance reverses the dictum of the rabbinic legend which seems to make religious devotion a matter of man's choice and man's seeking out God. Certainly the dictum of St. Augustine is true: "Our hearts are restless until they find their rest in thee." This highlights the Hebrew-Christian understanding of the ways of God with humankind. God is the initiator, not man. Man can only cry out.

Israel's second lesson from the Midian incident was that here at the beginning *a relationship was established*. First, a relationship between God, Elohim, and Moses who was receiving the call to lead. Just prior to the recorded conversation, Moses had experienced the strange phenomenon of the unconsumed burning bush. Was this merely an attention-getter for that which was to follow? Or was it, rather, a little epiphany to inculcate in Moses an initial trust relationship? A relationship that would be sorely needed later when the burden of leadership would become overwhelming.

Moses needed assurance, as does every leader who embarks upon a venture of faith. Let us put ourselves in Moses' place. Here is one who had been reared in Pharaoh's court, knowing all the privileges of living in the lap of luxury, yet by now having developed a social conscience that would cause him to use force, even murder, in a zealous attempt to right a wrong he witnessed. Then he would flee to escape the punishment for his crime. His was scarcely the kind of background experience to engender trust in anyone, and so, the episode of the burning bush. Once the initial relationship was established and Moses had reached the stage of acceptance, he needed some word to reassure those whom he would lead, and so the question: "If I go to the Israelites and tell them that the God of their forefathers has sent me to them and they ask me his name, what shall I say?" (Exodus 3:13, NEB)

Here we begin to deal directly with the relationship between authority and valid leadership. It was well-known in Israel that there were false prophets intermingled with the true. It has always been so and still is in the twentieth-century. Witness the plethora of the self-ordained whose false leadership has preyed upon the gullible merely for self-aggrandizement or for profit. Moses' leadership needed authentication so that there would be no question among those he would lead. When God called, Moses' first answer "Who are you?" was most important.

At this point in the story, its most important element is introduced. *God reveals his covenant name.* In all of Scripture the name sets forth the character of its bearer and here for the first time a new name for God revealed, Yahweh, along with the statement "This is my name forever and thus I am to be remembered." (Exodus 3:15b)

So much is involved in the use of this name. Although untranslatable, the new name for God, Yahweh invokes the sense of mystery regarding the one whom it represents. It is significant that to man was given the responsibility to "name" the creatures of the earth, but only God names himself, and in that name is the concept of eternity. God is Lord of the past, present and future.

Because the name of God is to be remembered forever, it has important implications for daily life. In the decalogue the command "Thou shalt not take the name of the Lord thy God in vain" has usually been interpreted to mean "don't curse, swear, etc." However, if we look deeper, we perceive that it also involves the warning against emptiness of lives that do not include God, especially on the part of those who claim a faith-relationship. In some circles Christian baptism is spoken of as a "Christening," taking the name of Christ. Especially it's true when the newly converted in our mission fields adds a Christian name to indicate the establishment of a new relationship apart from the former life. How sad it is when there are those whose subsequent lives do not reflect the taking of a new name.

It is this same command that echoes in the petition of the Lord's Prayer "Hallowed be thy name" and which prompted Luther to interpret: "God's name is indeed holy in itself, but we pray in this petition that it may be hallowed by us also." (Luther's Small Catechism)

Some seventy years ago Martin Buber, the great Jewish philosopher-theologian, produced a little book entitled: "Ich und Du," which was mistranslated "I and Thou." Perhaps this mistranslation was fortunate, as it brought to many who read it an understanding of God as the eternal "other," who at the same time revealed himself as "person" to be addressed and to bear a relatedness to creation, including all of nature and mankind. As one is confronted by the eternal "Thou" how can there be any response except the sense of awe and reverence!

It is precisely at this crucial juncture in Jesus' ministry, dealing with the sons of Israel, that he identified himself as one with God the father with the same words God gave to Moses at Midian: "Before Abraham was 'I am.'" Little wonder then that the official leaders became so angry with him when he used this most holy name to identify himself.

Exodus 12:1-14   Proper 13[1]

Remember Toward the Future
John M. Cobb

... *'This day shall be for you a memorial day,*[2] *and you shall keep it as a feast to the Lord; throughout your generation you shall observe it as an ordinance forever."*

(v. 14)

Dear friends,

Today, beginning this week, we here in Canada have a most special week, and that is because tomorrow is a special holiday, namely "Heritage Day." And by that is meant *that* day, or week, where one remembers *especially* his or her *national* or *ethnic* heritage. . . .

It is, indeed, interesting the way that we *have* these holidays in Canada: First, in the month of May, there is Victoria Day — where especially the British[3] think back to *their* golden age under Queen Victoria.

Then, in the month of July, there is Canada Day, where we can consider the fact that we are all Canadians.

And then, finally, as a rather *new* holiday — and, I have to say, still not 100% established[4] — we have *Heritage* Day — where everyone can remember where he or she comes from, and what he or she brings along *as* a *heritage*: Scots, Ukrainians, the French, the Chinese, and, yes, also the Germans.

Thus, *this* day is, especially for us, especially for us gathered here — of *very great importance* — because, for my part, after *some* experience in the area of history, I am convinced that *we* still have something to contribute — indeed, that we have a *lot* to contribute. And, indeed, to both groups: to the Church in Canada, regardless of which language she is speaking, and, also, to those people who identify themselves with German culture in Canada, whether they are Lutherans or not.

Yes, we have, perhaps, even more than *ever before . . . something* to *contribute*. But *why*? Why *today especially*? Because *somehow* the *conditions* of our *time* are *creating strong demands* within the *inner beings* of *people*.[5] For we live, indeed, in a perplexing and confusing time — We have everything; and we have nothing. We have great *possibilities*: *Technology* is highly developed; and the chances that our children might go to the university or to a good *technical* school — these are also great. But, on the *other* side: Our children *today* can hardly learn *anything* by memory anymore: Not the catechism, not the Bible verses, nor our proverbs, nor our church hymns, nor the folk songs,[6] nor the stories of the past — the way it was once done.

Yes, it seems *true* what I heard expressed a week ago in the *Ideas* program of the CBC: "We are, today, actually one of the *poorest* cultures in *history . . .* We have *everything* in the area of technology, but next to *nothing* in the head." That is, *no oral tradition* to pass *on* to the *next generation*.[7]

. . . Everything in the computer and nothing in the head . . .

Thus, when a human being has nothing — and I mean in *reality* nothing, although he might think that he has everything — when something essential is *lacking* there, then that person becomes *restless*, and there gets to be an *inner desiring* — for *what* exactly he does not know.

People today are *searching* for something, but they don't know exactly what *for*.

I've heard that a person can also see something like that in animals, in livestock. For example, when there is a deficiency in a trace mineral, such as phosphorus for the bones,[7] or magnesium, or, in our area, selenium, then that animal can have a lot of feed, the nicest looking *hay* and this and that, but *still*, there *is something lacking*. And he gets restless, and I have *heard* that some go around and even chew on *tree* trunks. Crazy behavior, isn't it? But, if you know that something *essential* is *missing*, and can't be *gotten* just by normal eating, *then* that funny behavior makes *sense*!

Thus, *today*, people are searching also in the *past* because there is the *feeling* that something from the *past* is *missing*.

And — this thing becomes more serious. Familiar to some of you, I'm sure, is our Provincial Archives. That is, in Edmonton, that place where they have all of these old documents. And it is fact that in the past several *years*, many, many people have been busy researching their family *trees*. *That* is, *today*, a *big phenomenon* and *thousands* of people are doing it. But this matter gets yet more serious. I have a friend at the archives, who has been working there for several years now. And, over the years he has *noticed* just how the number of researchers has been increasing: People, who are looking for their great grandfathers and great grandmothers. But *today, today*, there is a new phenomenon: Especially moving, he says, are, today, the *children* who come to the archives to *search* for their *parents*.

We have, today, everything; and we have nothing.

On the one hand, we have computers which can hold hundreds of names, and, on the other children who must come to the Provincial Archives to find out who their parents are!

Thus, Heritage Day — a time, when we can remember where we *come* from, and what we have brought *with* us, and what we have to *contribute*. And we can be *thankful* to our government, that some people there have been able, in a public manner, to *point* our searching into a healthy *direction*.

Because people are going to *search* no matter what. Some will seek that missing element in the *Shopping* Mall. Or some, in the *drug* culture. Others, however, will come to the *insight* that the *problem* lies in the *profound loss* of a *religious tradition*, for, yes, we all have the Bible — that, certainly — But, how do you know what is *in* it? How do you *understand* all of those things that are there? And, yes, here we are sitting in a fine church.⁹ But who built it? And, what was their *purpose*, their *intention*? And, what did they *want* for their children and grandchildren?

Dear friends, these Lutheran congregations that we have in western Canada, they have *not* come to be *just* by *chance*. It was not just by *chance* that the French Catholics settled in *St. Albert*, that the Ukrainian *Orthodox* were in the Vegreville area, and that the German *Lutherans* were at *Ellerslie* (at that time Lutherhort) and here at *Gnadenthal*. *That* was *not just chance*. No, that was an *intention* of people who believed: that they would act, that they would *do* something, that they would *build* something, and *that*, if *possible*, they would do these things according to the *will* of God.

Thus, we can be thankful to our government, that with Heritage Day we are pointed into a good direction.

Now, Heritage Day, that is not *the* answer. It is *not* the "last word," for we still have the *question*: But what *is* actually our heritage? But, at least, we are pointed in a *good direction*.

For, I wouldn't go looking around too *much* in the Shopping Mall; *and* I wouldn't go looking at *all* in the drug culture. But, if a person, for example, begins to look into a *French* heritage — then *perhaps* that person might find *God* in the Catholic Church. And, if a person, for example, begins to look into *Ukrainian* culture — then *perhaps* that person might find *God* in the *Orthodox* Church. *And, if* a person, for example, begins to look into *German* culture, it *may* be that *perhaps* that person might find *God* in the *Lutheran* Church.

But, *not* necessarily.

When I was in school (many of the professors were not Christian; and further, I had the feeling that for *some* of them, the *church* was an embarrassment) that somehow the relationship was not good. We heard *much* about Goethe and Schiller and Hegel and Nietzsche, but not a great deal about *Luther* and, I think, in eight years, scarcely *one word* about *Paul Gerhardt*.

Yet, even there, where many were *not* Christian, I shall still have to say: It was in German class where I learned "A Mighty Fortress" by heart, not in the Sunday school. And it was in the German lessons that I also learned something of what a real *church* bell does: "Strongly anchored in the ground stands a form of hardened clay . . ."[10] (Friedrich Schiller) And a person could go on: For example, it is from the American Historical Society of Germans from Russia[11] (Edmonton chapter) where today I hear the most about our brothers and sisters in Siberia (people who now, finally, under Gorbachev are receiving permission to emigrate).[12]

Thus, Heritage Day and our heritage: There *are* possibilities to *come back to the Christian tradition*, and I would want to say *especially* here in Canada where *our* forefathers were mostly Christian.

Thus, now, I want to get to the matter at hand and say something — a little — about our Christian forefathers, and then about what the Bible has to say to us. In the end, the Bible must have the last word.

So, to begin with, that fact that there *are* Lutheran congregations in Ellerslie, Hay Lakes, Rollyview[13] and Gnadenthal — is not simply by chance!

The people at *that* time, the time of settlement, *those* people (that is, the people who wanted to stay in the church — those who didn't always go to Calgary and get a job)[14] showed *three major characteristics. Three* special *things characterized* their way of *life*, and I want to name each of them:

1. First, they knew where they came from. They knew that they were Christians, and they knew that they were Lutherans. Bible verses, church hymns, the liturgy, and the catechism — these things they knew from memory. These things were *in* the memory and in the heart. *This* was *not* "the poorest culture in history," as some have called ours today! Rather, these people *had* something which they could pass on to their

children. Thus, the people of that time lived *from* a tradition, but they also lived *into* the future.

2. *Second*, our forebears *wanted* to *stay together*. They wanted to be able to form a viable congregation.[15] The *government* at that time was not 100% in agreement. Earlier, in Manitoba, they had allowed the Mennonites to set up colonies on a legal basis (otherwise the Mennonites would not have *come* from Russia). And, somehow, they also allowed the Icelanders by Lake Winnipeg to form a colony with some self government. But later — 1890, 1900 — some German Lutherans also tried it; and the government did not want, officially, to say "yes."

Those, at *that* time, had little interest in congregations; they had more interest (on the part of the CN and CPR[16]) in land sales, in wheat harvest, and in selling farm machinery.

Thus: "Why don't you spread out a bit more?"[17]
"Why don't you go along with the rest of *society* a bit more?"
"You can harvest *just* as much grain!"

But, *somehow*, our fathers managed to do it anyway: *settled* so that their *people* stayed *together*, so that they could form *good, viable* congregations. Not so much by legal means, but *rather* by help for the immigrants, by encouragement here and there so that most of them *could* stay together. Thus, our ancestors: 1. knew where they came from (and brought along a living *Lutheran*, a *Christian* tradition);
2. wanted to stay together; and
3. (now) wanted to *do* something; They wanted wanted to *build* something.

Oh friends, that is so important for a Christian person that he or she does not come into church with a sour face as if it were a *burden* to show up here on Sunday morning, but, rather, cheerfully, because the *Christian wants* to *do* something.
Dear friends,

Last September, we were gathered in the German Interest Conference of our church in Philadelphia. And there we elected

our president, and afterwards he said to me: "John, I am really busy — the congregation in New York and also the work in New Jersey — that is a lot. But I accept this office because *I want to do something.*"[18] "Because I want to *do* something." That was like music to my ears, for that is an *important part* of being a Christian. The *Christian* wants to *do* something. And for our *ancestors, too*, this *was* the case. *They, too*, wanted to *do* something. And, according to their means they *did* do a *lot*. Thus for *us, too*, for us who are sitting here today — we, *too*, should be wanting to *do* something:
> That is a part of being a Christian.
> That is like the good fruit that the
> *tree* wants to make our good works.

And the doing, *that* doing, comes from *life*.

But *what, what* to do and *how*? What should *we be doing today*?

And here, now, I want to finally return to our sermon text, to the Word of God, to that story of ancient Israel. For the people of Israel *also* wanted to do a lot; and they *did* do a lot. You will remember: How the people came into Canaan,
> and conquered the land,
> and made the land fruitful,
> and built houses and schools, and a
> wonderful temple. All of that
> *they did.*

But *first* of all God told them: "*This* you should do and *not forget.*[19] "on the tenth day of this month [you] shall take ... a lamb ... your lamb shall be *without blemish* ... [And] the whole assembly of the congregation shall kill their lambs in the *evening* ... [You][20] shall eat the flesh that night roasted; with unleavened bread and bitter herbs ... And you shall let none of it *remain* until *morning*, anything that remains until the *morning* you shall *burn*."

Note all of these details, the instructions!

And then, further, verse 14:

> "*This day shall be for you a* memorial *day, and you shall* keep *it as a feast to the Lord; throughout your generations you shall observe it as an ordinance for ever.*"

And further, verse 24:

"You shall observe this rite as an ordinance *for* you *and for* your sons *for* ever."

And when you come to the land which the Lord will give you, as he has promised, you shall keep this service.

And when your children say to you, 'What do you mean *by this service?' you shall say, 'It is the sacrifice of the Lord's passover, for he passed over the houses of the people of Israel in Egypt when he slew the Egyptians but spared our houses.'*
. . . And the people bowed their heads and worshiped.

Do *you* want to *do* something? If *so*, then you must go *back*, must return to *origins*, to the *foundation*, to *God* and, indeed, to God as he has revealed himself in the *past*. That's the way it was for the ancient Jews and that's the way it must be for *us* Christians *today*! For we Christians have *our* Passover, as well — and that which *we*, too, must do.

For our Lord Jesus has taken the *old* Passover and has put *himself* there in place of the lamb. *That* is, for *us*, now, the *Lord's Supper*. And this, *too*, with the *same command*: "Do this in remembrance of me." That *means*, now:

> If you intend to *do* anything with your life, *today*,
> then you must also go *back* into the past,
> *back* until you come to the *right foundation*,
> back until you come to *God* and to his *grace*.

"*Seek* and you will *find*". . .
For only where you experience the grace of God,
there where he *frees* us — *not* especially from Egypt, but more,
> from *sin*,

from *death*, and from the *devil, throughout* the *world* — Only when you return and come to the *Cross*, and can thankfully receive what *God* has done for *you*, only *then* can you again put your *life* in order, only *then* can *you* really do the *right thing*. Amen

NOTES

¹This sermon, with only slight modification, is a translation from the original German delivered on July 31st, 1988, at Grace Lutheran Church, Gnadenthal (RR#1, Leduc), Alberta. Americans wishing to incorporate these ideas into their own sermons may wish to focus on the Fourth of July and other American national holidays.

²In Luther's German, literally, "You shall have this day for the memory."

³"Die Briten," colloquial in Canada for those (also in Canada) of more pronounced (European) British origin.

⁴The writer has seen this day designated on some Canadian calendars simply as "Civic Holiday," although the Heritage Day theme seems to be quite strong in Alberta.

⁵"im inneren Menschen," literally "in the inner man."

⁶Volkslieder

⁷The quote is for purposes of homiletic style. Actually, the statements are paraphrased and "a week ago" is only approximate.

⁸Likely more than a trace, properly speaking.

⁹Built, as I understand it, in the 1940s, it is a late example of the nineteenth-century Gothic revival, outstanding for that area and time in Alberta.

¹⁰"Fest gemauert in der Erden steht ein Form aus Lehm gebrannt" is the opening line of Schiller's "Lied von der Glocke" describing the scene where the church bell is to be poured. Printed in its entirety in the June/July 1987 issue of *Kirchliches Monatsblatt* (Winnipeg), the editor, Hans-Martin Steinert, later noted that scarcely any other item drew so much response (both positive and negative) from the readership as the printing of this poem. (From comments at the German Lutheran Conference; Philadelphia, Pennsylvania; September, 1987; attended by the author.) In Schiller's work the church bell is seen (and heard) as it accompanies the villagers through a multitude of life-situations. Obviously an important sign of public Christianity, the era of Schiller's writing, on the other hand, was also a low one for the church itself in Germany. (See Conrad Bergendoff, *The Church of the Lutheran Reformation*, St. Louis: Concordia Publishing House, 1967, pp. 175f.)

¹¹Many in this congregation are descendants.

[13] In May of 1988 already a record, 30,000 are expected to have emigrated back to Germany by the end of the year. This is out of an estimated two million still living in the Soviet Union. (E. Schmidt, *Deutschland-Nachrichten* (Ottawa) (May 18, 1988, p. 3)

[13] Other places in Alberta not far from Gnadenthal, all a part of the same general settlement pattern.

[14] "Job." In German "Job" (pronounced somewhat as in English) has a negative connotation contrasted with "Beruf" (or "calling"). A person with a "Job" is working for money.

[15] "Gemeinden." The same word in German is used for both congregation and community which were often coterminous.

[16] Of course, that the railroads were not totally indifferent to the question of settlement patterns is evident by Robert England's book *The Colonization of Western Canada* (London: P.S. Kind and Son, Ltd., 1936). The point for homiletic purposes is the question of priorities.

[17] Quotations are for homiletic purposes only.

[18] Actually paraphrased.

[19] Emphases throughout this quotation are mine.

[20] A literal translation from the *Lutherbibel*.

Exodus 14:19-31   Proper 14

Exodus Crossings
— or —
When the Future Opens!
James G. Cobb

There is a story in which Moses is complaining to his public relations director that there is a lack of coverage in local Egyptian news media. Nothing seems to be getting the attention it should. And so, in conversation, the public relations director replies, "you are not getting the newspaper coverage you want, Moses, because you are not doing anything exciting."

Moses answers, "Very well. I shall go down to the Red Sea, wave my right hand, the waters will part, and the Hebrews will pass through safely. Then I will wave my left hand, the waters will return, and the pursuing Egyptians will be swallowed up."

The PR Director replies, "If you do *that* Moses, I can guarantee you four pages in the Bible."

And so, apparently, the PR person was able to deliver on the promise and the pages of the Book of Exodus see this event as the event of all Hebrew history.

How differently we would treat the account from Exodus appointed for today. Our summations would sound something like a network news broadcast in an attempt toward "objective reporting"; it might go something like this:

> *It was reported today that a band of Israeli refugees escaped across the border of Egypt. In an unexplained phenomenon,*

> the Israelies reportedly moved their entire company into and across the Red Sea. No casualties or deaths were reported. However, the Egyptian military unit charged with border security, drove heavy equipment into the same body of water and it is reported that they suffered a total loss of life and equipment. At this time there is no further information available from our wire services. We will update any new developments or further information.

To read the fourteenth chapter of Exodus is to lose all so-called "objectivity." There is no apology in this account. *The Exodus was deliverance and salvation to the Israelite!* It was the chronicle of their delivery from the hand of the oppressor. It was their salvation. Every narrator would recount this day in celebrations combining the emotions of our Fourth of July and national day of Thanksgiving. And the exultation exploded in thanks because of a confession of faith. For on that day, "the Lord saved Israel from the hand of the Egyptians." Never mind their protest when they stood on the shoreline and the water lapped at the hems of their robes. Never mind accusations against Moses that he had led them to this place to die. Never mind the presence of the "pillar of cloud" or the rod stretched forth from the hand of Moses. Never mind the attempts at explaining the unexplainable with walls of water held back and a dry path exposed as their gangplank. Never mind all that mystery and amazement, but do mind and give attention to their great confession and tribute. God, our God, saved us. Our God delivered us. Our God goes before us and comes behind us. Great is this God, our God, and greatly to be praised.

So this is the deliverance event of salvation for the Hebrew. This is the event remembered and recalled, recited and celebrated. There was a time when God made a passageway out of oppression and opened the way to the promised future. Now whenever there was occasion to wonder "what has God done for me lately?" the answer would be, "God led my people out of Egypt. God delivered me out of the hand of the oppressor and saved me."

This passage is indeed a magnificent account. It is pivotal in Scriptures not only as *the main event* in Israel's history, but also as the confession of faith lifted up and celebrated as well. Consider the following:

First, God has a future for his people. Looking around at the pyramids, the slavery, the forced labor camps, one would have wondered. Is this people being punished? Why is God allowing such terrible conditions to be present in this world? Has God abandoned us completely? Time after time, the Scriptures lift up the chronicle of God preparing a future for his people; one which they cannot as yet see. In Israel's experience of slavery, God had a promise of freedom. When Israel experienced exile, God had a promise of homecoming. When Israel experienced what seemed to be the silence of God, God raised up a prophet to speak his Word.

Pastors in congregations often hear the stories of people who relate their stories of despair and hope. A student walks in to thank someone for helping with monies needed for college. They were going to try the year not knowing where the funds would come from or how they would make ends meet. Someone in the congregation wanted to help that student, knowing the problems in the family, and gifts were given to help. There was nowhere to turn, but somehow, a special gift through the congregation made the difference. "Thanks for the help," says the student. The future looked closed off but now it isn't! There's surprise in a gift of someone else's love and care.

A person comes to speak about the numbing shock of the "pink slip." It came with no warnings, no apparent reasons; a feeling of betrayal and abandonment; a feeling of powerlessness and pity. Could we share that information with some people? The network of relationships and contacts expands. After some weeks, a new offer comes, and while it was not from anyone within the congregation, the person is grateful and thankful for what numerous members in the congregation said and did during that time. "I never knew what support and help our people would be." It's a surprise to receive the outpouring of someone else's love and care.

The congregation gears for a new group of refugees. The family of four arrive with one small satchel of worldly possessions. They speak broken English and the eyes and lives can do nothing but trust and hope. They arrive at the apartment; the following days are filled with visits, orientations, driver's licenses, jobs. In the loneliness of exile and the despair of culture shock, the day comes when the "thank you" is spoken: "we came with nothing; we did not know what would happen. Thank you for your love and care." That future was once unknown; now it is filled with new life.

A person comes to visit a month after the death of a spouse. "We were together for sixty-four years. I thought when she died my life was over. It's so hard now to be without her; it's one day at a time, with tears that come unexpectedly. I don't know if I told her often enough how much I love her. I thought I couldn't go on. But I look around and think maybe I can help or talk to someone going through the same thing. God sure keeps us close even in death." God keeps us close and God opens a new future: a future not of our own making but one of his own gracious provision. God has a future for his people!

Second, God does not abandon or desert his people, rather we travel with him on our way. An anonymous writer has told a telling story in the popular account called "Footprints." A man dreams a dream in which he looks back at the path of his life. For most of his life, he sees two sets of footprints in the sand — his and the Lord's. But over the lowest moments of his life, he sees only one set of footprints. The man, feeling betrayed, questioned the Lord: "I don't understand why when I needed you most, you would leave me." The Lord's answer is "it was then that I carried you."

The theology of "Exodus" has become Good News for all people. The story is an ever present reminder of a God who delivers his people from the forces of slavery and oppression, sin and death. The Gospel is of a God who has a future for his people: life bestowing and life opening. The Gospel is of a God who accompanies his people and his creation never to desert or abandon even in the midst of the most desperate of all situations. And so, with the children of Israel, we celebrate the God who frees and delivers us, the God who sets before us a future full of promise and hope, and the God who accompanies us on our way. One of the most beautiful prayers in our worship speaks a summation of this text and passage:

> *Lord God, you have called your servants to ventures of which we cannot see the ending, by paths as yet untrodden, through perils unknown. Give us faith to go out with good courage, not knowing where we go, but only that your hand is leading us and your love supporting us; through Jesus Christ our Lord. Amen*
>
> (Lutheran Book of Worship, Augsburg Publishing House, Minneapolis: 1979, p. 153)

Exodus 16:2-15   Proper 15

When God Provides, It's a Manna Miracle
James G. Cobb

It was really an unusual story the one I heard that day. I was used to people occasionally coming in off the street to talk. Every day in parish ministry you never know what that particular day will be like. The woman, mid-thirties, came in and asked if I had just a few minutes to listen to her story. She said she didn't go to church and was not affiliated with any denomination. She was a school teacher and in her teachers' lounge at school a number of people mentioned our congregation and now she had to tell someone her story. She was the mother of a five-year-old son and about eight months earlier had gone through a divorce. She related how during the next weeks depression had set in and was getting worse. She found herself sitting alone in a dark room while her son watched television or played outside. There had been one night recently when she sat in the darkness and had thought very seriously of suicide. Lost in that thought, she said her son burst into the room, turned on the lights and said, "hey Mom, how about some popcorn?"

For some unknown reason, she explained, her son, the light, and his request changed everything there in that quick moment. Suddenly out of her depression she knew she had a son to live for and a blessing in life just for *her* in spite of her problems. And then she concluded, "I just wanted to tell someone 'thank you' and share the joy." The woman left and, by the way, her entry had been with conditions: she wouldn't tell me her name or her school and she made no promises about church or anything else and so, to this day, she remains an anonymous visitor. I believe she was directing her thanks to God for a life-line, for a blessing, for a rescue and for saving of her life!

In light of the Exodus text, real life continues to produce God's gracious provisions for our salvation. To this day I wonder if the woman ever had occasion to read or hear this story of the Israelites and whether she would ever consider her son's popcorn to be God's gift of manna for her? I know that the story of this strange visitor in my office has me remembering her account and that I even see "popcorn" as a referent to her conversation. I see some Lenten fairs use this product as another Easter symbol when the kernel of corn explodes into something delightfully different.

Occasionally even another story is told about this product, like the one I read recently from a Kindergarten teacher who wrote a song about popcorn. She would have students sit on the floor to sing it and then at the appropriate time, all the children would "pop" until they were standing. But one day the teacher noticed one child who stayed on the floor when all the others had popped up. "What's wrong?" asked the teacher, "why aren't you popped like the other children?" "Because," said the little boy, "I'm burning on the bottom of the pan."[1]

"Burning on the bottom of the pan" is easily an accurate description of the human condition. Through the Exodus, this condition is most often found in the summation of what is described as "murmuring" usually against Moses or Aaron or God. As soon as the stomach became empty and the mouth became dry, numbers of Israelites longed for the fleshpots of Egypt. How easy for food to become more important than freedom. The stories around the campfires would "drip" with sentiments about those "good ole days." While God was the guide and the leader of their present journey, they easily forgot

God as their present help and began to resent this hard pilgrimage. "So, where is God now?" they would cry. "Has God abandoned us and left us? Are we left here to die?" The people murmured and often they did not get what they expected.

One evening my wife and I were in the kitchen preparing dinner. Our two-year-old son had liked the taste of newly-discovered soft drinks. We had just poured a dark-colored beverage into small glasses on the table for dinner and we were aware of what had begun to happen. He had tiptoed in and taken a carrot off a platter. At his next trip, he saw the beverage poured and quietly lifted a glass from the table. I know he expected the sweet, sugary soft drink — instead we heard a gasp and a choking and spitting. He has discovered prune juice! Not quite what was expected; a lesson in "looks can be deceiving." We don't always get what we think we want! So, too, with the Israelites, when they were disappointed, they became angry. They did not mind ten plagues raining down upon the Egyptians, but you can bet they had some misgivings about setting out with one knapsack per person! They did not mind heading out toward a land of milk and honey, but they *did* mind an army of Pharoah's chariots bearing down on them. They did not mind the vision of a great new future, but they did mind the dust and dirt, the steep mountains and the dangerous ravines. They did not mind the dream of freedom, but they did mind the lack of food. They murmured. They were "burning on the bottom of the pan." Stomach rumblings were finding their way into verbal complaints.

At the very point where the people once again are dangerously close to falling off the edge, the story turns dramatically to speak of God's intervention. The Lord's Word and action combine to proclaim "I will provide." The quail-bird and the manna-bread will again be a sign of the Lord's caretaking for this his people. They will know provision instead of poverty and food instead of famine.

The story of the Exodus provisions of God is not a story so easily relegated to the past. Among the faithful it is often a summation spoken as a confession or doxology to God. A distraught single parent came in to the church office seeking help for an apartment deposit. She had a new job, a child, but needed this help. We could only provide a portion; still we were interested in how others would help. I asked her to call us next week with what happened. A number of churches and people came through. In her need, she proclaimed simply, "God provided."

An aged parishioner has an aching wound over the death some years ago of their young, vigorous son in an automobile wreck. Often in attendance at funerals, and especially during Lent and Easter, the parishioner says through the tears, "God provides for me. What promises in Jesus' victory over death."

If there is one unique mindset for the Hebrew in the Old Testament, it is vision to "see" the God who is in, with, under, beside, around and beyond everything. The very role of Moses and Aaron was in connecting word and event and act, conversation, prayer and intercession to God on behalf of the people and from God back to the people. The Book of Exodus knows God in plague and pestilence, fiery cloud and Red Sea, burning bush and mountain cloud, bitter water and sweet manna. In events and experiences, in words and wonders, in deeds and in daily duties, "God provided!" And into the present tense for you and me: *God provides.*

Elizabeth Barrett Browning expressed such insight:

> *earth is crammed with heaven and every common bush afire*
> *   with God.*
> *But only he who sees takes off his shoes,*
> *the rest sit round it and pluck blackberries.*[2]

Do we see? Does God provide?

God provides our life. He may save us with popcorn, a meal, a word, a world hunger offering, a kindness of a person never forgotten, an apartment deposit, quails or manna. But these are still the minor gifts. The greatest gift is God himself. The One who chooses not to abandon us but to accompany us all the days of our lives. He has come to teach us to pray to the One who alone is the source and giver of "our daily bread." He has come to offer us forgiveness and life, and God speaks with word and gift and says, "take and eat, this is my body given for you for the forgiveness of sin." Yes, God provides. He provides with signs along the way until we are finally with Him who is the Way. The Way through all the entanglements of this world's wilderness. He is the Way. He is the Provider.

---

[1] Voicings Publications, *Sunday Sermons*, (Margate, New Jersey: July/August, 1988), p. 29.

[2] Elizabeth Barrett Browning, "Aurora Leigh"

Exodus 17:1-7
(Mark 4:35-41)

Proper 16

The Cry for God
James G. Cobb

It was early evening and time for the little boy to go to bed. But outside, the sky had turned dark with clouds rolling in, then lightning flashes and a series of explosive thunderous booms. The father tucked his son under the covers and said, "you'll be all right; just go to sleep now."

The encouragement worked until the next boom of thunder . . . then the patter of feet on the floor and a call from the top of the stairs. "Daddy, I'm scared."

The father came upstairs again; he thought that this might be a time and occasion to talk of God, and so came the father's wise words, "now when you're scared, just remember God is with you, too. There's nothing to be scared of."

The encouragement worked until the very next boom of thunder and again, he heard the sound of feet scampering across the floor: "Daddy, I'm scared!"

"Do you remember what I told you?" asked the father.

"Yes," said the little boy, "I know God is with me; but I'd like someone who has skin on."

Yes of course, the child is asking to be held, embraced, and comforted. And there is an asking that is more than words, ideas, or pious platitudes. It is a search for a person, the personal or a personality. It is a cry for God so often lifted up epecially out of the depths in times of trouble. I suspect that everyone here has uttered the words at some time or other,

"God where are you?" The cry for God is universal, even to the atheist or the nonbelievers. The question comes across the consciousness sometimes, somewhere, "God, if you are, where are you?" And God has heard that cry raised up over the thousands of years.

When the people of Israel were on the move, having come through the Red Sea and led on their way by God out of Egypt, the time came at Masseh and Meribeh when they were thirsty; and because they were in great want of water, they accused God of abandonment. In the seventeenth chapter of Exodus, they tempt the Lord with their question and ask, "Is the Lord among us or not?" This cry to God has gone up early in the history of God's people and it continues . . .

The cry for God would be echoed by the Psalmist who would talk of a time when his life was filled with troubles, where tears have covered his face day and night; and, in Psalm 42 he says his neighbors have been his accusers continually "so . . . where is your God?"

In the Book of Job, Job has had it with his troubles and in the thirtieth chapter he, too, becomes God's accuser saying, "God has cast me into the mire and I have become like dust and ashes . . ." and then to God, "I cry to you and you do not answer me, I stand before you and you do not give me any attention." The cry has gone up again.

In the fourth chapter of St. Mark's Gospel, with the winds on the Sea of Galilee whipping the waves into violent churnings, the disciples, with Jesus present in their midst, wake him and scream out, "Teacher, do you not care if we perish?" This crying out to God, spoken and screamed out at God, has continually been a pulse beat across the pages of Scripture and will find its way into your life, too, if it has not already. Sometime and in some place, you too will ask, "God, where are you? Do you not care?" Even the humanity of Jesus cries in intercession from the Cross, "my God, my God why have you forsaken me?"

We sound out our cries to God in the midst of trouble, pain, illness, guilt, and brokenness. And yet, if we go back to the miracle story from St. Mark, we are reminded that a little faith is enough. There are none of us who think we have such great and solid faith that we will never be scared and frightened and knocked off balance. Martin Luther once wrote a sermon on this passage and commented that "great faith doesn't need Christ's assurance or presence. Great faith stands before God without need of the support or the strength of a Savior." But little faith, "little faith" writes Luther, "needs a Christ." He comments, "if the faith of the disciples had been strong, they would have said to the sea and the waves: 'beat against us as you may, your forces are not strong enough to overthrow our boat, for Christ our Lord is on board with us,' but the disciples had only a little faith, but they invested their little faith in a big Lord and that is why they were not destroyed."[2]

In my years of ministry, I continue to hear the excuse that people won't come to church because it is full of hypocrites. Of course it is! We are the ones who acknowledge our sin, who know our weaknesses, our hypocrisies, our complete inability to save ourselves. We are the ones who admit our little faith. We are not a people of great faith, but we bring what little we have and what little we are to a Lord who is so greatly sufficient. And even like the Israelites, the Psalmist, and Job, we can bring our anger, our fear, our accusations, and our skepticisms to a God who is sufficient.

Out in the boat, in the midst of a life-threatening situation, the disciples took their little faith to Jesus and then in the second part of this brilliant account, what happened? Richard Hoefler comments that they might have expected Jesus to pray to God. Of course they knew and had Jesus in the flesh; they called him "good teacher." But Jesus stood up, not this time in prayer, but with command and authority, he spoke a rebuke to the winds and the sea. To the surprise of all the disciples, Hoefler writes, "Jesus acted like God and spoke like God" and the flailing forces[3] there, even of nature obeyed him. They were awed and now even shocked or fearful in a new way, exclaiming unto themselves, "Who is this that even the winds and the sea obey him?" The word from St. Mark's Gospel leaves no doubt: this is the God who has come to live and dwell among us; this is God in the flesh, God incarnate in Jesus Christ. Now, in our fear, like the little boy in the thunderstorm, we have someone with skin on. We have someone who is the Word and speaks and acts with authority. This is our Lord.

Yes indeed, this is our Lord: the One who today has spoken a word with such awesome power that it forgave and erased your sin and mine. Do you hear that word spoken in our worship when God announces that your sin is forgiven?

This is our Lord: One who in Baptism, speaks a word with water poured on the head of an infant and thereby makes this child his very own! Do you hear and grasp that word?

This is our Lord: the One who hosts a table, forgives his people and grants them a foretaste of the feast to come: Do you hear his promise spoken to you with the bread and wine?

This is our Lord: the One who does not walk away from his own suffering and death, but trusts God to redeem and transform the whole ugly mess into our salvation. Do you see this faith underway in Him for our sakes?

This is our Lord: the One who said, "Lo, I am with you always even to the close of the age." This is the One about whom St. Paul wrote in Romans, "nothing in all creation can separate us from the love of God in Christ Jesus." Nothing: not an extreme failure, not a disappointment, not a diagnosis or a depression, not even our own hypocrisy or our own little faith; no, not even death will separate us from the love of God in Christ Jesus.

Across the pages of our Holy Scriptures, what trail-markings God has left! Trails through Egypt and Judea, through Masseh and Meribeh and onto mountains called Sinai and Transfiguration and Olives; through the Red Sea and the Sea of Galilee and the River Jordan. We see the trail-markings through Cana weddings and funerals from Nain and preachings in Capernaum. We see power released in changed lives of tax collectors, prostitutes, soldiers, and children. We see trail-markings across dinner conversations and banquet feasts and last suppers. We see trail-markings in brutal executions and an empty tomb . . . all trail-markings inviting us to faith!

When the boat we are in is swamped, when the waves are beating us to death, when life seems wrenched away, when we cry out for God: there is One who has spoken with authority even to the cosmic forces of creation, and there is One who has acted in order to save. He is Jesus Christ. And you and I are the people of his faithful and abiding care. May this peace of Christ which passes all understanding keep your hearts and minds through all storms, and yes even through accusations, questioning, rage, and anger toward God when you too scream out: "Is the Lord among us or not?"

---

[1]Richard Hoefler, *There are Demons in the Sea*, Lima, Ohio: The C.S.S. Publishing Company, Inc., 1987, p. 102.
[2]*Ibid.*
[3]*Ibid.*, p. 106.

About the Authors

James G. Cobb: grandson of the Rev. William G. and Lillian Akard Cobb; son of Rev. James K. Cobb; graduate of the College of William and Mary; Lutheran Theological Seminary at Gettysburg, Pa. Doctor of Ministry degree from Gettysburg. Parishes served: St. Martin, Annapolis, Maryland; Christ, Fredericksburg, Virginia; Trinity, Grand Rapids, Michigan. Presently a member of the Church Council, Evangelical Lutheran Church in America and pastor of First Lutheran Church, Norfolk, Virginia.

James K. Cobb: son of the Rev. William G. and Lillian Akard Cobb; a graduate of Lenoir-Rhyne College and Lutheran Theological Southern Seminary. Parishes served: St. Andrews-St. Michael, Columbia, South Carolina; Reformation Taylorsville, North Carolina; Philadelphia, Granite Falls, North Carolina; Rader, Timberville, Virginia; Messiah, Knoxville, Tennessee; Immanuel, Blountville, Tennessee; Emmanuel, Roanoke, Virginia; Our Saviour's, Norge, Virginia; Good Shepherd, Goldsboro, North Carolina; Faith, Newberry, South Carolina. Presently retired in Newberry, South Carolina and serving as supply in various congregations.

John M. Cobb: grandson of the Rev. William G. and Lillian Akard Cobb; son of the Rev. John W. Cobb; graduate of the University of North Carolina; Waterloo Lutheran Seminary at Waterloo, Ontario. Ph.D. candidate, University of Manitoba. Parishes served: Trinity, Ponoka, Alberta; Evangelical St. Peter Kirche, Winnipeg, Manitoba; Teacher of Religious Studies and College Pastor, Camrose Lutheran College, Camrose, Alberta. Presently serving part-time, Grace Lutheran Church, Gnadenthal, Alberta, and completing dissertation work.

John W. Cobb: son of the Rev. William G. and Lillian Akard Cobb; a graduate of Lenoir-Rhyne College and Lutheran Theological Southern Seminary; D.D. degree: Lenoir-Rhyne College. Parishes served: Trinity, Rocky Mount, North Carolina; Luther Memorial, Blacksburg, Virginia; Grace, Bethlehem, Pennsylvania; Holy Trinity, Raleigh, North Carolina. Presently retired and serving as Executive Director of Lutheran Men of North Carolina, Statesville, North Carolina.

Judith A Cobb: married to James G. Cobb; graduate of Upsala College and Lutheran Theological Seminary at Gettysburg, Pennsylvania. She is an Associate in Ministry certified by the E.L.C.A. in Educational and Youth Ministries. She has served in that capacity at Trinity, Grand Rapids, Michigan, and presently at First Lutheran, Norfolk, Virginia. She serves on the E.L.C.A. Division for Ministry.

John D. Mauney, Jr.: married Mary Emma Cobb, daughter of the Rev. William G. and Lillian Akard Cobb. Graduate of Lenoir-Rhyne College and Lutheran Theological Southern Seminary; D.D. degree: Lenoir-Rhyne College. Parishes served: Mt. Olive, Hickory, North Carolina; St. James, Fayetteville, North Carolina; Shepherd of the Hills, Sylva, North Carolina. Presently retired in Cherryville, North Carolina and serving as supply and vice-pastor of various congregations.

W. Dexter Moser: married Elizabeth Cobb, daughter of the Rev. William G. and Lillian Akard Cobb; graduate of Lenoir-Rhyne College and Lutheran Theological Southern Seminary. Parishes served: Kure Memorial, Kure Beach, North Carolina; Mt. Moriah, China Grove, North Carolina; Shades Valley, Birmingham, Alabama; Redeemer, Houston, Texas; St. Mark, Corpus Christi, Texas; Program Director, Lutheridge Camp and Conference Center, Arden, North Carolina; Bethany, Memphis, Tennessee; Secretary, Southeastern Synod, L.C.A. Presently retired in Cherryville, North Carolina and serving as supply and vice-pastor of various congregations.

www.ingramcontent.com/pod-product-compliance
Lightning Source LLC
Chambersburg PA
CBHW060847050426
42453CB00008B/866